CIRCLING THE GLOBE

A Guide to Countries and Cultures of the World

RAINTREE
STECK-VAUGHN

CIRCLING
THE
GLOBE

A Guide to Countries and Cultures of the World

Volume 8
Southern and Eastern Asia

RSVP

**RAINTREE
STECK-VAUGHN**
P U B L I S H E R S

The Steck-Vaughn Company

Austin, Texas

General Editor Sue Grabham
Senior Coordinating Designer Tracy Killick

Editors Claire Berridge, Jane Butcher,
Charlotte Evans, Nina Hathway, Ann Kay,
Linda Sonntag, Jill Thomas
U.S. Editor Emily Kent
Assistant Editor Julia March
Editorial Assistant Virginie Verhague

Cartographer Alan Whitaker
Cartographic Editors
Tara Benson, Annabel Else
Assistant Cartographic Editors
Nicola Garrett, Victoria Hall
Cartographic Services
Cosmographics, Lovell Johns Ltd.
Base Map Artwork Malcolm Porter

Senior Designer Janice English
Designers Paul Calver, Dawn Davies,
Earl Neish, Andy Stanford
Additional Design Branka Surla, Smiljka Surla

Additional Art Preparation Shaun Deal,
Roy Flooks, Mark Franklin, Matthew Gore,
Mel Pickering, Janet Woronkowicz

Writer Linda Sonntag

Picture Research Su Alexander, Elaine Willis
Artwork Archivist Wendy Allison
Assistant Artwork Archivist Steve Robinson

Publishing Director Jim Miles
Art Director Paul Wilkinson

Production Manager Linda Edmonds
Production Assistant Stephen Lang
U.S. Production Manager Oonagh Phelan

Indexer Hilary Bird
Glossary and Phonetics Daphne Ingram
Proofreader Penny Williams

Geographical Consultants
Keith Lye, Dr. David Munro
Natural History Consultant
Michael Chinery
Social Geography and History Consultant
Professor Jack Zevin

KINGFISHER

Larousse Kingfisher Chambers Inc.
95 Madison Avenue
New York, New York 10016

First American edition in ten volumes published
1995 by Raintree Steck-Vaughn Publishers, an imprint of
Steck-Vaughn Company, P.O. Box 26015, Austin, TX 78755

LIBRARY OF CONGRESS CATALOGING-IN-PUBLICATION DATA
Circling the globe.—1st American ed.
p. cm. Includes index
Contents: vs.1. and 2. Europe—vs.3. and 4. Africa—v.5. North America—
v.6. South America—vs.7. and 8. Asia—v.9. Australia and the Pacific Islands—
v.10. Ready reference and index.
1. Geography—Juvenile literature. (1. Geography.)
G133. C4B 1995 910dc20 95-21696 CIP AC

ISBN 0-8172-4082-9

Printed in Italy

2 4 6 8 10 9 7 5 3 1

8

SOUTHERN AND EASTERN ASIA

USING THE MAPS

The box below contains a map key. It explains what the different symbols on the maps in this encyclopedia mean. For example, a square marks a capital city, and a black line marks a road. On the right is a sample map. The lines of latitude and longitude are marked in degrees. The letters and numbers between the lines are the grid references. They help you to find places on the map by identifying the square in which they are found.

The scale bar on a map helps you to measure distances. On this map 0.87 inches equals 200 miles and 0.5 inches equals 200 kilometers.

The town of Antserañana is marked by a circle. The circle is in grid reference B1. To find it, all you have to do is look down the map from B and across the map from 1.

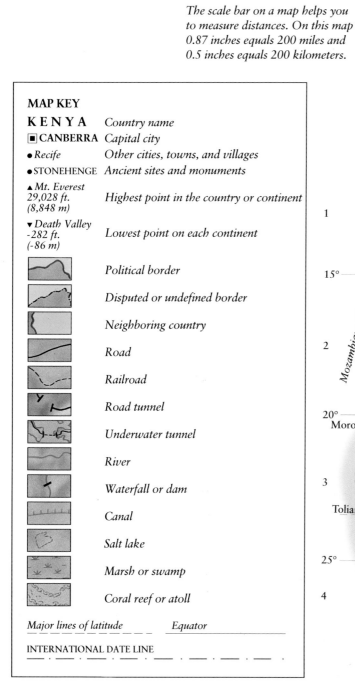

MAP KEY

K E N Y A	*Country name*
■ **CANBERRA**	*Capital city*
● *Recife*	*Other cities, towns, and villages*
● STONEHENGE	*Ancient sites and monuments*
▲ *Mt. Everest* 29,028 ft. (8,848 m)	*Highest point in the country or continent*
▼ *Death Valley* -282 ft. (-86 m)	*Lowest point on each continent*
	Political border
	Disputed or undefined border
	Neighboring country
	Road
	Railroad
	Road tunnel
	Underwater tunnel
	River
	Waterfall or dam
	Canal
	Salt lake
	Marsh or swamp
	Coral reef or atoll

Major lines of latitude _____ *Equator*

INTERNATIONAL DATE LINE

MALDIVES

The Maldives are a string of tiny tropical islands lying in the turquoise waters of the Indian Ocean. There are about 1,200 islands altogether, but only 200 are inhabited. They are low and flat, many only just sticking up above sea level.

White sandy beaches line the shores and brilliantly colored fish such as the poisonous scorpion fish dart among the coral of the clear blue lagoons. Some islands have no vegetation, but on most, coconut palms and breadfruit trees grow in shallow soil. At dusk, giant fruit bats called flying foxes glide between the trees.

Sinhalese people sailed west from Sri Lanka to settle the islands around 500 B.C. The Maldives became trading posts for the Portuguese and Dutch from the 1500s, then were ruled by the British from 1887 until independence in 1965. Fishing provides a major source of the islanders' income. Bonito, the main catch, and other fish are exported to Sri Lanka and Japan. Pineapples, pomegranates, and yams are grown here, but rice has to be imported.

Tourism is by far the fastest-growing industry. Many of the resorts are foreign-owned, but increasingly islanders are developing their own resorts. Local crafts, such as shell necklaces and carved wooden fish, are sold to tourists.

▼ This aerial view shows that the Maldives are formed from coral reefs. Coral are tiny underwater animals, some of which live inside chalky skeletonlike structures. These structures build up into a rocky deposit. Sometimes they stick out above the water and form an island.

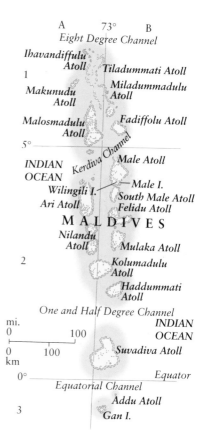

A 73° B
Eight Degree Channel
Ihavandiffulu Atoll
1   Tiladummati Atoll
Makunudu Atoll   Miladummadulu Atoll
Malosmadulu Atoll   Fadiffolu Atoll
5°
INDIAN OCEAN   Kerdiva Channel   Male Atoll
Wilingili I.   Male I.
Ari Atoll   South Male Atoll
Felidu Atoll
M A L D I V E S
Nilandu Atoll   Mulaka Atoll
2   Kolumadulu Atoll
Haddummati Atoll
One and Half Degree Channel
mi.   INDIAN
0   100   OCEAN
0   100   Suvadiva Atoll
km
0°   Equator
Equatorial Channel
Addu Atoll
3   Gan I.

FACTS AND FIGURES

Area: 115 sq. mi.	**Official language:** Divehi
Population: 238,000	**Main religion:** Islam
Capital: Male, on Male Island (56,000)	**Currency:** Rufiyaa
	Main export: Fish
Highest point: On Wilingili Island (79 ft.)	**Government:** Republic
	Per capita GNP: U.S. $500

PAKISTAN *Introduction*

Pakistan is an Islamic republic in southern Asia. Along its northeastern border with China, the high peaks of the Karakoram Range form a desolate barrier of ice and stone. By contrast, the neighboring northern territory of Jammu and Kashmir is a beautiful land of lakes and mountains. Ownership of part of this region is disputed with Pakistan's neighbor, India. In the northwest a road climbs the lonely heights of the Khyber Pass, a narrow passage through the mountains to Afghanistan. To the west a dusty highway leads to southern Iran. In the southwest little grows on the dry and rocky Baluchistan Plateau, while the sandy wastes of the Thar Desert stretches into the southeast from India.

The center of Pakistan is a great plain called the Punjab, which means "five rivers." It is called this because the plain is watered by the Indus River and its four major tributaries, the Jhelum, Chenab, Ravi, and Sutlej. The Punjab is extremely hot and dry, but a vast irrigation system allows the cultivation of wheat, rice, cotton, and sugarcane. During the occasional violent rainstorms that occur, the irrigation channels help prevent serious flooding. They catch the water that might otherwise wash away the crops. The Punjab's rivers are also used to harness hydroelectric power at dams such as the Tarbela Dam on the Indus River.

Pakistan has many industries that produce cotton, carpets, sugar, and processed foods. These goods are transported between large cities such as Rawalpindi, Lahore, and Karachi by road and rail.

FACTS AND FIGURES
Area: 307,372 sq. mi.
Population: 122,802,000
Capital: Islamabad (201,000)
Other major cities: Karachi (5,103,000), Lahore (2,922,000) Faisalabad (1,092,000), Rawalpindi (928,000)
Highest point: K2 [Dapsang] (28,250 ft.)
Official language: Urdu
Main religion: Islam
Currency: Pakistani rupee
Main exports: Cotton and cotton goods, rice, leather, carpets, fish
Government: Islamic republic
Per capita GNP: U.S. $410

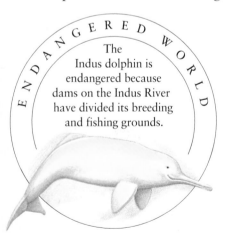

ENDANGERED WORLD

The Indus dolphin is endangered because dams on the Indus River have divided its breeding and fishing grounds.

▶ *Boats line the docks in Karachi's fishing harbor. The Arabian Sea yields an immense array of fish, including sharks and several kinds of herring. Pakistan exports large quantities of fish and shellfish.*

450

▶ Irrigation brings water to the Punjab, the flat plain in the center of Pakistan. This allows rice to be grown in flooded paddies, which would otherwise be dusty and dry. Farmers also grow wheat and raise goats in this region. They use oxen to help them till the soil.

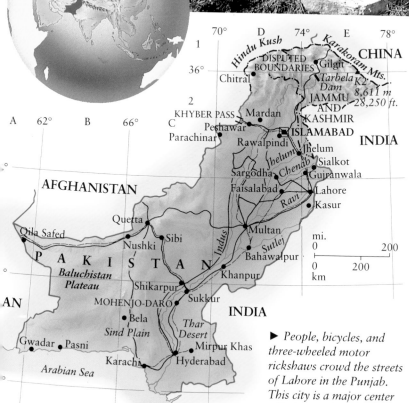

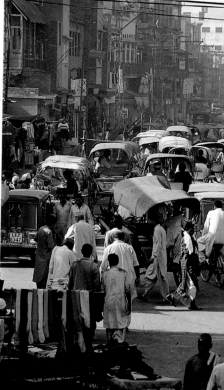

▶ People, bicycles, and three-wheeled motor rickshaws crowd the streets of Lahore in the Punjab. This city is a major center of industry, banking, culture, and education.

PAKISTAN *People and History*

One of the world's first great civilizations flourished in this land around 2000 B.C. The peoples of the ancient Indus empire settled in the Indus Valley and produced fine architecture and pottery. Over the next 3,500 years, the area was invaded by Arabs, Greeks, Persians, and Turks. The British gradually took over India during the 1800s, and by 1900, this included all the lands that are now Pakistan. From the early 1900s, however, India wanted to be independent from Britain. At the same time tensions increased between the two main religious groups—Muslims and Hindus.

When India eventually won its independence in 1947, two separate Muslim areas in northwest and northeast India became the country of Pakistan (meaning "Land of the Pure"). Muslims from all over India moved to the new country while most Hindus stayed in India. In 1971, civil war broke out between East and West Pakistan. The eastern half renamed itself Bangladesh, while the western half became modern-day Pakistan.

Since the 1970s, the army has repeatedly seized control of the country, but Pakistan has also had periods of democratic rule. In 1988, Benazir Bhutto was elected the Islamic world's first woman prime minister. Many Pakistani women, however, still do little work outside the home and are veiled in public. Some Pakistani men dress in Western-style clothes, others wear the traditional long shirt and baggy trousers called *shalwar-qamiz*. Many are farmers who grow crops such as rice and sugarcane.

▲ *A potter puts the finishing touches to a teapot in Peshawar, near the Afghan border. Pakistan has a long tradition of fine craftwork, which also includes carpet making, leather tooling, and metalwork.*

◀ *This classroom is crowded with boys from the Sind Plain. There is no law that says children must be educated and few girls are sent to school. Most adults are unable to read or write, though the children of wealthier families may study at one of Pakistan's 24 universities.*

◄ Worshipers crowd in front of the great Badshahi mosque in Lahore, built in 1674. The people of this land were converted to Islam by Arab invaders around A.D. 700. Modern Pakistan is a strongly Muslim nation.

► Ruins of the city of Mohenjo-Daro show that it was one of the earliest examples of a planned city. The streets were laid out according to a grid and were well drained. It was an important center of the Indus civilization, which flourished in Pakistan about 4,000 years ago.

◄ Boys in Faisalabad get ready to ride on the roof of a crowded bus. Pakistanis take pride in decorating their buses, trucks, and vans with pictures, mottoes, slogans, colored lights, and chains.

453

मसमेव जयने

INDIA *Introduction*

India is the seventh largest country in the world and it has the second largest number of people. This vast land contains contrasts of every possible kind—in peoples, languages, customs, religions, and landscapes. There are massive mountain ranges covered permanently by ice and snow, vast plains crossed by broad rivers, a parched desert, dense tropical forests, and palm-fringed beaches.

Many of these places can be reached within hours by plane. However, most travelers use the crowded buses or trains, and journeys can take days. Passengers cram onto the seats, often sharing space with chickens, goats, and other animals that are being taken to market.

About three-fourths of India's vast population live in rural areas, where most people are farmers. Crops of rice and wheat are grown in the fields, and animals are kept on small plots of land. However, in recent years thousands of people have moved away from this traditional life to find work in the cities. Life is very different away from the countryside. Noisy crowds fill the narrow city streets and rickshaws thread their way through the traffic. The larger cities are now major industrial centers as India continues to make great progress in science, technology, and industry.

▲ *The Taj Mahal, near the city of Agra, is a tomb. It was built in memory of Mumtaz Mahal, the wife of the Muslim ruler Shah Jahan. The tomb was constructed from gleaming white marble. It took 20 years to build and was completed in 1653.*

FACTS AND FIGURES

Area: 1,222,237 sq. mi.
Population: 896,567,000
Capital: Delhi (8,400,000)
Other major cities: Bombay (12,596,000), Calcutta (11,022,000)
Highest point: Kanchenjunga (28,208 ft.)
Official languages: Hindi, Assamese, Bengali, Gujarati, Kannarese, Kashmiri, Malayalam, Marathi, Oriya, Punjabi, Sanskrit, Sindhi, Tamil, Telugu, Urdu, Nepali
Main religions: Hinduism, Islam, Christianity, Sikhism
Currency: Indian rupee
Main exports: Gems and jewelry, clothing, cotton, textiles, tea, engineering goods
Government: Multiparty republic
Per capita GNP: U.S. $310

◀ These three-foot (1-m)-high string puppets come from the Jodhpur region. Puppets like these have been tales of love and bravery for hundreds of years.

▶ Pedal rickshaws, streetcars, and people jostle for space in Calcutta. This is the most crowded city in India, with over 78,000 people per square mile (2.6 sq. km).

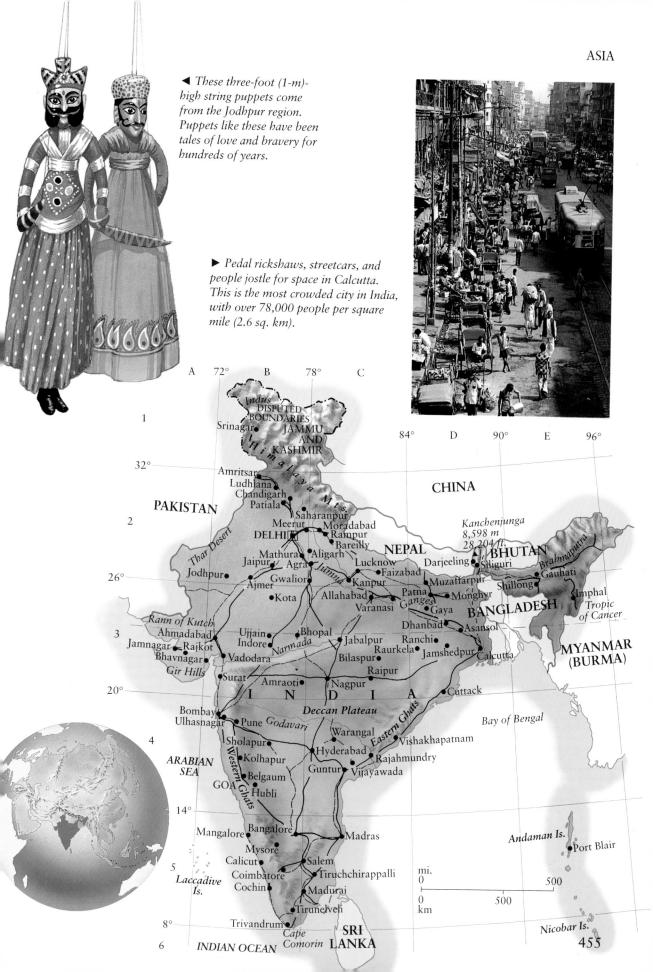

A 72° B 78° C

1

Indus
DISPUTED
BOUNDARIES
Srinagar JAMMU
AND
KASHMIR

84° D 90° E 96°

32° Amritsar
Ludhiana
Chandigarh
Patiala

PAKISTAN

Saharanpur
Meerut Moradabad
2 DELHI Rampur
Bareilly

CHINA

Thar Desert

Mathura Aligarh Lucknow
Jaipur Agra Faizabad
Jodhpur Gwalior *Jumna* Kanpur
Ajmer Kota Allahabad Patna
26° Varanasi *Ganges* Gaya

NEPAL

Kanchenjunga
8,598 m
28,204 ft.
Darjeeling Siliguri BHUTAN
Muzaffarpur *Brahmaputra* Gauhati
Monghyr Shillong
BANGLADESH Imphal
*Tropic
of Cancer*

Rann of Kutch
Ahmadabad Ujjain Bhopal
3 Jamnagar Indore *Narmada* Jabalpur Ranchi
Rajkot Vadodara Bilaspur Raurkela
Bhavnagar Dhanbad Asansol
Gir Hills Surat Amraoti Nagpur Raipur Jamshedpur Calcutta

MYANMAR
(BURMA)

20° I N D I A Cuttack

Deccan Plateau

Bombay
Ulhasnagar Pune *Godavari*
4 Sholapur Warangal *Eastern Ghats* Vishakhapatnam
Western Ghats Kolhapur Hyderabad Rajahmundry

Bay of Bengal

ARABIAN
SEA Belgaum Guntur Vijayawada
GOA Hubli

14° Mangalore Bangalore Madras

Andaman Is.
Port Blair

Mysore
Calicut Salem
5 Coimbatore Tiruchchirappalli
*Laccadive
Is.* Cochin Madurai

mi.
0 500

0 500
km

Tirunelveli
8° Trivandrum
*Cape
Comorin* SRI
LANKA

Nicobar Is.

6 INDIAN OCEAN

INDIA *Geography*

The great triangle of India points down into the Indian Ocean. It occupies most of a huge landmass that, along with Bangladesh and Pakistan, is often called the Indian subcontinent. Along the top of the triangle run the magnificent snowy peaks of the Himalayas, some of the world's highest mountains. The beautiful slopes and lakes of Jammu and Kashmir nestle in the northwest of this mountain range. India and Pakistan are in dispute over who should control the region. The foothills of the Himalaya Mountains are covered in forests where leopards and tigers roam.

To the south of the Himalayas lie the wide Northern Plains. The majority of the population lives here, in fertile areas such as the huge flood plain of the mighty Ganges River. The arid wastelands of the Thar Desert stretch away to the west.

Moving farther south, the third major region of the country is

▼ *The towering Himalaya Mountains separate India from central Asia and China. Melting snow from their ridges and glaciers feed the Ganges River. Both the mountains and the Ganges are sacred to the Hindus, who make up most of the population of India.*

the great plateau of the Deccan, which makes up most of central and southern India. This giant plateau includes farming and grazing land. It is also rich in mineral deposits. The Deccan is bordered on either side by the mountains and hills of the great Western and Eastern Ghats, which drop down to coastal plains. The Western Ghats are higher than the Eastern Ghats, and large parts of its foothills are covered in tropical rain forest. The west of the country catches the full force of the summer winds each year, which bring heavy monsoon rains to the whole of India.

▶ *Wild elephants wade in the lake at the Periyar Wildlife Sanctuary in the south. The park also protects antelopes, monkeys, wild boars, tigers, and large deer called sambars.*

▶ *Sandy beaches lined with coconut palms form the coastline of Goa, a popular tourist spot. Goa is India's smallest state. It is affected heavily by the monsoon rains, which sweep across the country from June to September.*

▼ *Camels make their way across the fiercely hot, empty sands of the Thar Desert. Little of this region can be cultivated, although crops such as millet, sorghum, and corn grow on the irrigated edges of the desert.*

▶ *Tea grows on the hills of Darjeeling. The climate in these Himalayan foothills seems cool in comparison with the heat of the plains to the south.*

INDIA *Economy*

India is a land rich in natural resources and produces vast quantities of food and manufactured goods. However, the rapid growth of its population means that there is still not enough food for everyone. Many of India's people remain extremely poor, and natural disasters such as severe drought, earthquakes, and floods often add to their hardship.

The country has huge expanses of farmland, but much of it is not naturally fertile. Since India gained its independence in 1947, a great deal has been done to modernize farming practices, and today agriculture contributes about one-third of the country's income. Various irrigation projects have been developed to bring water to dry areas. Experiments with new types of seeds and fertilizers have also resulted in much bigger harvests. Despite this, most farms are too small for modern machinery and can produce only enough food to feed one family. Farms in India are getting smaller all the time. This is because, under Hindu law, land is divided equally among the children on their parents' death. Some people want to reform this law so that farms can be much larger and more productive.

Since the 1950s, industry has transformed India's cities. Heavy machinery and electrical goods are now manufactured alongside traditional products such as cotton and silk. Plentiful supplies of oil and coal provide power for the factories and generate more than half the country's electricity.

Service industries are also growing in importance and more Indians are working in tourism, banking, and communications.

ECONOMIC SURVEY

Farming: Most farms are small and grow food crops such as rice, wheat, millet, and beans. Mangoes, nuts, tea, jute, sesame seeds, and spices are produced. Sixty-two percent of the population are farmers.
Forestry: Cedar, teak, and rosewood are felled for timber.
Fishing: Mackerel, sardines, and shrimp are caught in the sea. Carp and catfish are fished in the rivers.
Mining: Iron, coal, oil, mica, manganese, and diamonds are extracted.
Industry: Textiles, iron and steel, machinery, and electronic goods are produced. Craft products include jewelry, leather, carpets, and metalwork.

▲ *A potter shapes clay on the wheel in a scene that has changed little in thousands of years. Other traditional crafts include metalwork, weaving, and fabric printing. These items are exported all over the world.*

▼ *Traders crowd an alleyway as shoppers haggle over the prices of vegetables and spices in a typical Indian market.*

◄ Steel is processed at a mill in Jamshedpur. The metal is used in the manufacture of cars, trucks, buses, bicycles, industrial machinery, electrical goods, and domestic appliances such as sewing machines.

► Women carry rubble from a building site. Much of the heavy work in cities and on farms is still carried out using muscle power rather than machinery. Many of the hardest jobs tend to be done by the lowest caste (social class).

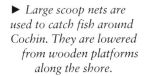

► Large scoop nets are used to catch fish around Cochin. They are lowered from wooden platforms along the shore.

INDIA *People*

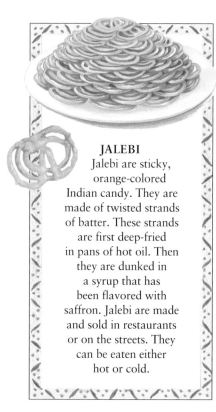

JALEBI
Jalebi are sticky, orange-colored Indian candy. They are made of twisted strands of batter. These strands are first deep-fried in pans of hot oil. Then they are dunked in a syrup that has been flavored with saffron. Jalebi are made and sold in restaurants or on the streets. They can be eaten either hot or cold.

India is a country with many different ethnic groups and around a thousand languages and dialects. There are also a large number of religious faiths, although more than four-fifths of the population is Hindu. According to Hindu tradition, people are born into social classes called castes. Strict religious rules govern the food, clothing, and jobs of each caste.

Family ties are very important in India and marriage is often seen more as a union between two families than a relationship between two people. It is the custom for parents to choose their children's marriage partners for them. Today, some Indians are trying to break down these social rules by encouraging young people to pick their own husband or wife.

In India's many villages, the way of life has not changed much in centuries. People fetch their water each day from the village well and light their homes with paraffin lamps. As the economy continues to grow, more villages have access to plumbing facilities and electricity.

In the cities, large numbers of people live crowded together in slums, while many wealthier Indians choose to live in areas that show a strong Western influence. Some people wear Western clothes, while others prefer traditional dress, such as the bright saris worn by many Indian women. Indian social life centers on the marketplaces in the towns and cities. They are full of people exchanging news and views amid the blare of pop music, the honking of car horns, and the shouts of street vendors.

◄ *Hindu children stand covered in colored water and dye as they celebrate the spring festival, Holi. During this festival people splash colors everywhere. They also play tricks on each other in memory of the mischievous behavior of Krishna, one of the Hindu gods.*

◀ Posters show popular Indian film stars. India's enormous film and video industry has gained a worldwide reputation. So many films are produced in Bombay that it has been given the nickname "Bollywood." Films are a favorite form of entertainment throughout the country, and popular subjects include love stories and dramas.

SPEAK HINDI

Hello—नमस्ते
(*nah - mah - stay*)

Good-bye—अलविदा
(*al - vee - dah*)

Please—कृपया
(*crew - pah - ya*)

Thank you—धन्यवाद
(***dan** - ya vad*)

Yes—हाँ   (*hah*)

▼ Traditional costume is worn for Kathakali *dancing in southwestern India. The dances tell stories about the lives of Hindu gods and demons. They are accompanied by chanting and drumbeats.*

▲ Poor people struggle to survive on the streets of Calcutta. Above their shelters, a bank advertises saving plans that none of them could ever afford—there is a huge gap between rich and poor in this country. Most Indians live in villages, but many have moved to large cities such as Calcutta, Bombay, and Delhi in search of work that is not available.

461

INDIA *History*

One of the world's greatest ancient civilizations sprang up in the valley of the Indus River. Here, from around 2500 B.C., the Dravidian peoples developed an advanced economy and system of government. The Aryan peoples invaded northern India and pushed the original inhabitants south around 1500 B.C. It is mainly from these two peoples that Indians are descended.

India has seen the rise and fall of several great empires founded on religion. From 272 to 232 B.C., Emperor Ashoka ruled most of India and encouraged the Buddhist faith. By A.D. 400, under a family of rulers called the Guptas, Hinduism was enjoying a golden age. Muslim invaders conquered Delhi in 1192, and their rule spread across the north, while a powerful Hindu state called Vijayanagar flourished in the south. In 1526, a Muslim leader called Babur founded the empire of the Mughals (Mongols) in the north. The Mughal emperors became fabulously rich. Emperor Shah Jahan used some of his wealth to build the lavish Taj Mahal at Agra in the 1600s.

At this time, European traders began to gain a foothold. By the 1800s, the British East India Company controlled large areas, and in 1858, India became part of the British Empire. Demands for self-rule grew during the 1920s and 1930s, with a peaceful campaign organized by Mahatma Gandhi. When India gained its independence in 1947, Muslim territories in the northeast and northwest became the new nation of Pakistan. Since then India has experienced conflicts over religion and language, but it has remained the largest democracy in the world.

▼ *A splendid procession makes its way through the streets of Delhi on Republic Day, January 26. India became a republic in 1950. Independence from Britain is also celebrated each year on August 15.*

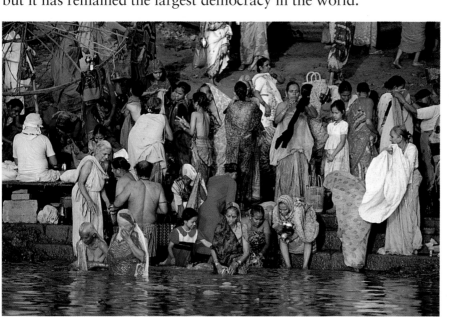

◄ *Hindus gather at dawn to bathe in the holy waters of the Ganges River at Varanasi. Hinduism has shaped Indian society since ancient times. Its sacred scriptures are believed to date back over 4,000 years.*

► *The Golden Temple is in the city of Amritsar. It is the holy place of the Sikh religion, founded in the 1400s by Guru Nanak. He instructed his followers to live a good and simple life. Today there are about 14 million Sikhs, many of whom live in the northern state of Punjab.*

▼ *This model of a tiger eating a European was made for Tipu Sultan of Mysore in the late 1700s. He fought many battles against the British East India Company.*

MAHATMA GANDHI

Mohandas Karamchand Gandhi was born in India in 1869. A believer in peaceful protest, he headed the successful campaign for Indian independence, using marches and hunger strikes. Gandhi led a simple life and became known as Mahatma, which means wise and holy leader. He was assassinated in 1948.

NEPAL

▼ *This is the temple of the Hindu god Krishna in Kathmandu. There are thousands of beautiful Buddhist and Hindu temples in this deeply religious country. The capital is especially famous for its temples.*

The Himalaya Mountains cover most of Nepal and form a snowy wall along the northern border with China. Their highest peak is Mount Everest, the tallest mountain in the world. Far below the icy peaks, rhododendrons cover the mountain passes of the Himalayan foothills. To the south of the mountains lies the humid and fertile Tarai plain, where rhinoceroses and tigers roam.

Most of the people of Nepal are farmers, using traditional methods to grow sugarcane, rice, corn, and wheat. Others herd sheep and yaks. Some work in tourism, since Nepal's spectacular landscape attracts mountaineers and trekkers from all over the world. Tourism has brought much needed money and development to this poor country. However, these changes are also threatening the local farmers' way of life and the environment. A cloud of pollution now hangs over Nepal's capital, Kathmandu. Also, more than one-third of the forests has been cut down since the 1950s. Both locals and tourists use the timber for cooking and heating. Poster campaigns encourage everyone to conserve resources.

From the late 1700s to the start of the 1990s, Nepal was ruled as a dictatorship, either by a monarch or by members of the powerful Rana family. In 1991, King Birendra gave up his powers. Free elections were held, which brought in a democratic government.

FACTS AND FIGURES
Area: 56,826 sq. mi.
Population: (21,086,000)
Capital: Kathmandu (419,000)
Other major city: Biratnagar (131,000)
Highest point: Mt. Everest (29,028 ft.)
Official language: Nepali
Main religions: Hinduism, Buddhism
Currency: Nepalese rupee
Main exports: Grains, jute, timber, oilseeds, clarified butter, potatoes, herbs, hides
Government: Constitutional monarchy
Per capita GNP: U.S. $170

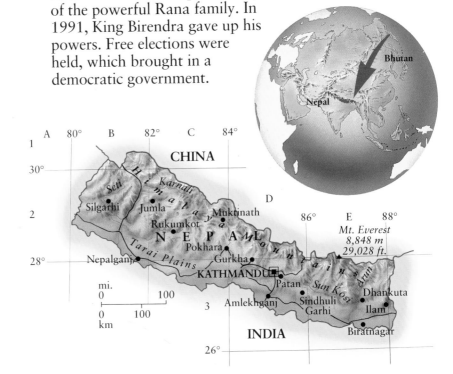

BHUTAN

This small country calls itself the "Land of the Thunder Dragon," the mythical beast that appears on its flag. Bhutan is protective of its centuries-old cultural traditions. Television is banned and the people are required by law to wear national costume. Both tourism and mountaineering are limited. Most of the people of Bhutan are Buddhists of Tibetan descent. Another important group is Nepali-speaking Hindus.

This is a land of extremes. Bananas grow on the humid plain that borders India, and forests of oak cover the cool central hills. In the north, the rugged Himalaya Mountains lie permanently under ice and snow.

The country came under Tibetan rule in the 1500s. From the 1800s, it was protected by Britain. In 1949, Bhutan became independent, although it placed the management of its foreign affairs in India's hands. India helped to build roads, develop hydroelectric power, and mine coal. However, Bhutan remains a basically agricultural country. Long-haired oxen, called yaks, are herded in the high mountain ranges. Farmers grow crops such as potatoes, citrus fruits, barley, wheat, and rice in the country's rich, fertile valleys.

FACTS AND FIGURES
Area: 17,954 sq. mi.
Population: 1,650,000
Capital: Thimphu (31,000)
Highest point: Kula Kangri (24,777 ft.)
Official languages: Dzongkha, English, Nepali
Main religions: Buddhism, Hinduism
Currency: Ngultrum
Main exports: Timber and wood products, coal, rice, oranges and apples, distilled spirits, talc, cement
Government: Constitutional monarchy
Per capita GNP: U.S. $180

[Map of Bhutan showing: CHINA to the north, INDIA to the south. Locations include Kula Kangri 7,554 m. 24,783 ft., Lingshi, Himalaya Mts., Punakha, Tongsa Dzong, S. Lao, Paro Dzong, THIMPHU, Ha Dzong, Sankosh, Wong Chu, Shongar Dzong, Kuru, Manas, Tongsa, Chhukha, BHUTAN, Kenga, Tashi Gang Dzong, Dewangiri. Coordinates: 89° A 90° B 91° C 92°, 28°, 27°. Scale: mi. 0 50, km 0 50]

▶ *In the capital, Thimphu, young monks watch the Tsetchu festival. It is held in honor of a Tibetan saint. Bhutan has many spectacular religious festivals and dances.*

◀ *Traditional farmhouses cling to the mountainside above irrigated terraced fields. Communities like this are often isolated because they are cut off by the steep mountains.*

465

BANGLADESH

FACTS AND FIGURES
Area: 57,294 sq. mi.
Population:
122,210,000
Capital: Dhaka
(6,106,000)
Other major cities:
Chittagong (2,041,000),
Khulna (878,000),
Rajshahi (518,000)
Highest point:
Mt. Keokradong
(4,034 ft.)
Official language:
Bengali
Main religions:
Islam, Hinduism
Currency: Taka
Main exports: Jute, tea,
hides, clothes, leather,
newsprint, fish
Government:
Multiparty republic
Per capita GNP:
U.S. $220

Most of Bangladesh is flat, very low-lying land. Two great rivers, the Ganges and the Jamuna, join forces just west of the capital, Dhaka. The rivers spill into a maze of waterways along the Bay of Bengal and form the largest delta in the world. There are frequent floods in Bangladesh, which have drowned both livestock and people. The floods also wash away crops, causing famine. Some experts want to control these floods with several engineering projects. Others recommend setting up local projects to help people survive, such as building platforms on stilts where people can escape from the floodwaters.

Most Bangladeshis use the traditional tools and methods of their ancestors to farm the plain and fish its rivers. The men and boys of the family plant and harvest rice, tea, sugarcane, or jute. The women and girls usually look after the home and garden, where they tend pumpkins or spices. Rural families live mostly in villages of bamboo houses built on embankments of mud. Travel between villages is often by canoe. Fewer than one-fifth of Bangladeshis live in cities since housing and factory jobs are scarce.

This land was once part of the Indian province of Bengal. By the late 1940s, it had become the eastern half of Pakistan. In 1971, civil war broke out when East Pakistan fought to break away from the control of West Pakistan. India fought on the side of East Pakistan and helped it to become the new nation of Bangladesh. Since independence, there have been periods of military rule, but today Bangladesh is governed by a democratically elected parliament.

▲ *River water has flooded these homes near Dhaka. Bangladesh is a land of rivers, and when the torrential monsoon rains come, the rivers burst their banks. Over the years, millions of people have been drowned or made homeless by heavy floods. Flooding is made worse by the cyclones that often strike Bangladesh.*

ENDANGERED WORLD

The gharial is a relative of the crocodile. It is hunted for its skin, and its eggs are taken for food.

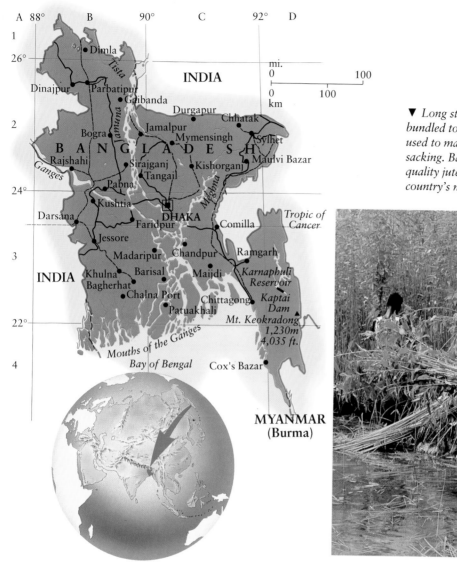

INDIA

mi.
0   100
0   100
km

B A N G L A D E S H

INDIA

Tropic of
Cancer

Mt. Keokradong
1,230m
4,035 ft.

Mouths of the Ganges

Bay of Bengal

Cox's Bazar

MYANMAR
(Burma)

▼ Long stems of jute are harvested and
bundled together. Its tough fibers are
used to make rope, matting, and
sacking. Bangladesh grows the best
quality jute in the world, and it is the
country's most important export.

◀ A Bangladeshi health worker holds a
clinic for mothers and babies. As part of
her job she may also advise villagers on
using clean water, preparing food
hygienically, and immunizing children
against disease. Health education is
particularly important in areas
devastated by flooding.

467

SRI LANKA

Sri Lanka is an island ringed with palm-fringed beaches. Inland is a fertile plain that rises through rolling hills planted with tea bushes to misty mountains. Rain forest covers the southwest.

In about 500 B.C., a Sinhalese prince from India conquered the Vedda people who were living here and called the country Sinhala. Around A.D. 200, the island was invaded again, by Tamil kings from India. The Tamils drove the Sinhalese into the south. The two groups continued to struggle for control of the country until the Portuguese arrived in the 1500s. They were followed by the Dutch and then the British, who ruled from 1802. The British called the island Ceylon. It became independent in 1948 and changed its name to Sri Lanka in 1972.

In the 1980s and 1990s, old tensions erupted again. The Hindu Tamils of the north resented being governed from the south by the Sinhalese Buddhists. Thousands were killed in guerrilla battles, and many Tamils left for India. However, throughout these troubles, Sri Lanka has held on to a basically democratic system of government. Peace talks in the early 1990s brought hopes of settling the situation.

About half of the population are farmers. Agriculture is the main economic activity, producing the important crops of coconuts, rubber, rice, and tea.

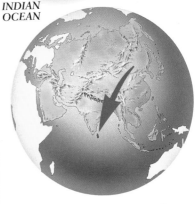

◄ The paddy-fields of Balangoda are surrounded by coconut palms. Beyond them forested slopes rise into the clouds. The forests are home to monkeys, elephants, and parakeets, while crocodiles lurk in the rivers. The rich beauty of the island inspired its name, Sri Lanka, meaning "shining land."

FACTS AND FIGURES

Area: 25,332 sq. mi.
Population: 17,619,000
Capital: Colombo
(588,000)
Other major cities:
Dehiwala-Mount Lavinia
(174,000),
Moratuwa (135,000)
Highest point:
Pidurutalagala (8,279 ft.)
Official languages:
Sinhalese, Tamil

Main religions:
Buddhism, Hinduism,
Christianity, Islam
Currency:
Sri Lankan rupee
Main exports: Textiles,
clothes, tea, gems,
rubber, coconut products
Government:
Multiparty republic
Per capita GNP:
U.S. $540

▲ *At Polonnaruwa, in central Sri Lanka, an ancient statue of the Buddha sits in calm meditation. It has been carved out of a single slab of granite. People leave flowers and rice cakes at its feet.*

▲ *A young woman goes shopping in the town of Jaffna. She wears the uniform of a Tamil Tiger, the guerrilla army that challenges the rule of the Sinhalese government.*

▶ *An elephant is dressed for a festival in Kandy. Elephants play an important part in Sri Lankan life. They take part in religious processions and work in lumberyards, where they are trained to carry logs with their trunks.*

MYANMAR (BURMA)

▼ *A Myanmar boy studies a holy book. Dressed in a monk's robe, he is one of many boys sent to monasteries to learn the teachings of the Buddha.*

Myanmar was called Burma until 1989. It is rimmed by forest-clad mountains that surround the broad valley of the Ayeyarwady River. Most of the population lives in the delta of this great river, where the houses are built on stilts to protect them from floods and wild animals. The delta is covered with rice paddies. Rice farming is the major occupation of the Myanmar people, but minority groups such as the Chin peoples live in the hills, where they survive by hunting and fishing.

The ancestors of today's population migrated down the Ayeyarwady River from Tibet and China, settling here from around 3000 B.C. Over the centuries, various empires held power in these lands. In the 1800s, the British moved in, and from 1885 until 1937, Burma was part of Britain's Indian Empire. Some years after full independence in 1948, the country began a period of military rule. The army closed the borders to the outside world, taking over schools and the running of newspapers. When people protested, many were shot or imprisoned. Meanwhile, rural areas were overrun by guerrillas. Some were led by warlords who traded in the illegal drug opium. In 1990, the country was in crisis and an election was called. The opposition party won, but their leader, Aung San Suu Kyi, was imprisoned by the military who continued in power.

Myanmar has rich natural resources of oil, gas, and precious gems, and in the 1990s it began to open up to foreign trade. However, some nations still refuse to deal with a government that does not respect human rights.

HTAMIN LE THOKE

Htamin le thoke consists of small dishes of leftovers such as rice, onions, potatoes, noodles, and spinach. Tamarind juice is poured over the top. This juice comes from the pods of the tamarind tree, which contain a reddish sweet-and-sour pulp.

▶ *Ruined Buddhist temples rise from the plain at the ancient Myanmar capital of Pagan. Founded in A.D. 849, the "City of a Thousand Temples" covered a vast area. It was partially destroyed by a Mongol army in*

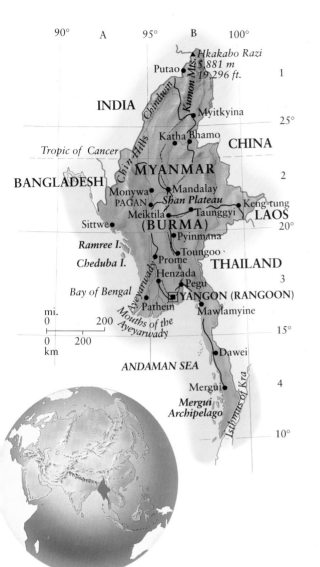

Area: 261,226 sq. mi.
Population: 44,613,000
Capital: Yangon
(Rangoon) (2,459,000)
Other major city:
Mandalay (533,000)
Highest point: Hkakabo
Razi (19,290 ft.)
Official language:
Myanmar

Main religions:
Buddhism, Christianity,
Islam
Currency: Kyat
Main exports: Teak, rice,
pulses, beans, rubber
Government:
Military regime
Per capita GNP:
Est. under U.S. $700

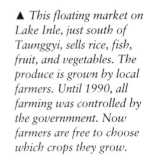
▲ This floating market on Lake Inle, just south of Taunggyi, sells rice, fish, fruit, and vegetables. The produce is grown by local farmers. Until 1990, all farming was controlled by the governmnent. Now farmers are free to choose which crops they grow.

THAILAND

Thailand (formerly Siam) stretches eastward from the fertile basin of the Ping Chao Phraya River across much of Southeast Asia. It is a land of rice paddies, mountains, and tropical beaches.

The Thais are descended from peoples who migrated from southern China between A.D. 200 and 1100. From the 1300s to the 1500s, Thailand fought wars with the Burmese, Malays, and Cambodians, but unlike its neighbors, it was never a colony of a European power. The Thais founded a kingdom with its capital at Bangkok in 1782. Descendants of the original royal family still rule today, but since 1932, real power has rested with the government. Modern Thailand has seen periods of military rule and political unrest. An elected coalition government was set up in the 1990s.

Many Chinese, Indians, and Malays, as well as the native Thais, live in Thailand. From 1970 to 1973, the country also became home to a million refugees from the Vietnam War.

Thailand's economy depends mostly on agriculture, and many people live by fishing or farming. The forests produce valuable teak, but the government banned tree-felling in the late 1980s. This was because large-scale felling had led to mudslides that killed hundreds of people. Manufacturing thrives in the cities, and industry is bringing increased wealth to Thailand. Tourism is also growing.

FACTS AND FIGURES
Area: 198,114 sq. mi.
Population: 58,584,000
Capital: Bangkok (5,876,000)
Other major city: Chiang Mai (165,000)
Highest point: Mt. Inthanon (8,511 ft.)
Official language: Thai
Main religions: Buddhism, Islam
Currency: Baht
Main exports: Rice, tapioca, manufactured products, machinery
Government: Monarchy, military rule
Per capita GNP: U.S. $1,840

KICK BOXING
Kick boxing originated in Thailand, and its popularity has now spread to other parts of the world. In this grueling sport, fighters use gloved hands, bare feet, elbows, and knees. The loser often ends up unconscious. There are 100,000 kick boxers in Thailand, both amateur and professional.

▼ *Strange limestone outcrops, like this one off Phuket Island, rise steeply from the blue waters around Thailand's coast.*

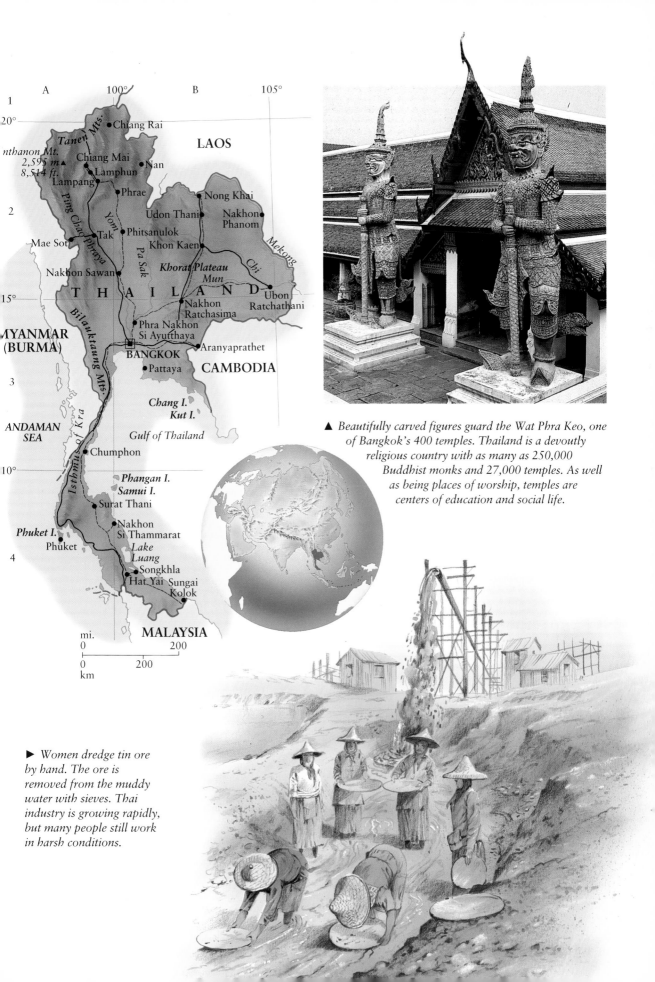

Map of Thailand

	A	100°	B	105°
1	20°		LAOS	

Tanen Mts.
Chiang Rai
nthanon Mt.
2,595 m
8,514 ft.
Chiang Mai
Nan
Lamphun
Lampang
Phrae
Nong Khai
Nakhon Phanom
Udon Thani
Mae Sot
Tak
Phitsanulok
Khon Kaen
Yom
Pa Sak
Ping
Chao Phraya
Nakhon Sawan
Khorat Plateau
Mun
Chi
Mekong
T H A I L A N D
15°
Ubon Ratchathani
Nakhon Ratchasima
MYANMAR (BURMA)
Bilauktaung Mts.
Phra Nakhon Si Ayutthaya
BANGKOK
Aranyaprathet
Pattaya
CAMBODIA
3
Chang I.
Kut I.
ANDAMAN SEA
Isthmus of Kra
Gulf of Thailand
Chumphon
10°
Phangan I.
Samui I.
Surat Thani
Phuket I.
Phuket
Nakhon Si Thammarat
Lake Luang
4
Songkhla
Hat Yai Sungai Kolok
mi.
0   200
0   200
km
MALAYSIA

▲ Beautifully carved figures guard the Wat Phra Keo, one of Bangkok's 400 temples. Thailand is a devoutly religious country with as many as 250,000 Buddhist monks and 27,000 temples. As well as being places of worship, temples are centers of education and social life.

► Women dredge tin ore by hand. The ore is removed from the muddy water with sieves. Thai industry is growing rapidly, but many people still work in harsh conditions.

CAMBODIA

Cambodia is a land of low plains and forested hills. It has a warm tropical climate, fertile soil, and plentiful monsoon rains, which make it ideal rice-growing country. Most of Cambodia's population live in farming villages and work in rice paddies.

Nine out of ten Cambodians belong to the Khmer peoples. Between the 800s and the 1300s, the Khmer built up a great empire across much of Southeast Asia, with its capital at Angkor. By the 1400s, Khmer power had weakened and a Thai army captured Angkor in 1431. A small Khmer kingdom existed until the 1800s. Cambodia was ruled by the French from 1863 to 1953, apart from five years of Japanese occupation during World War II.

During the Vietnam War (1957–1975), Cambodia tried to remain neutral. However, bitter fighting between United States troops and Vietnamese communists spilled across the border. There were years of fighting before the Khmer Rouge, a political party led by Pol Pot, seized power in 1975. This new dictatorship forced town dwellers to farm the land, and millions of people died of hunger and disease or were murdered. Both industry and farming collapsed.

In 1978, Vietnam invaded Cambodia and helped to overthrow the Khmer Rouge government. Unrest continued as the Khmer Rouge fought against the new Vietnamese-backed government. Democratic elections were held in 1993, and the monarchy was restored, but the Khmer Rouge continued their efforts to regain power.

FACTS AND FIGURES
Area: 69,898 sq. mi.
Population: 9,308,000
Capital: Phnom Penh (800,000)
Other major city: Battambang (45,000)
Highest point: Phnom Aural (5,947 ft.)
Official language: Khmer
Main religions: Buddhism, Islam
Currency: Riel
Main export: Rubber, rice, pepper, timber
Government: Constitutional monarchy
Per capita GNP: Est. under U.S. $700

▼ This poster was put up in Phnom Penh by the Khmer Rouge, who ruled the country from 1975 to 1978. It shows an ideal state with happy farm workers. In reality, Khmer Rouge rule was very brutal.

▲ These single-story houses, at a village near Siem Reap, are typical rural homes. They are built on stilts because flooding is common across Cambodia. Their walls may be made of bamboo, wooden planks, or palm leaves.

▲ A smiling god looks out from the tower of the Bayon, a monument at the center of the ancient capital of Angkor. This city was once the biggest in the world. Its temple, called a wat, is the largest religious building ever recorded.

◄ In the capital's rush hour traffic, passengers are crowded onto a rickshaw pulled by a motorcycle. Bicycles and motorcycles are the most popular forms of transportation. Few Cambodians can afford cars.

LAOS

Laos lies at the heart of Southeast Asia. Much of it is steep and rugged mountain country cloaked in dense forests. The majority of the population are farmers living along the fertile plains of the Mekong River. They cultivate corn, rice, coffee, and tobacco. Others work in the forests, which yield valuable woods such as teak. Trained elephants are used in these forests to move tree trunks. The few industries in Laos include tin refining and footwear manufacturing. Another source of income for the country is hydroelectric power, which is generated by a dam on the Mekong River and sold to Thailand.

From the 1400s to the 1700s, Laos was a powerful state known as Lan Xang, the Kingdom of a Million Elephants. It later split into separate kingdoms. In 1893, the area came under French rule, joining with its neighbors to make up French Indo-China. During the 1950s, French rule in Southeast Asia collapsed and northern Laos was invaded by communist rebels called the Pathet Lao. In the 1960s and 1970s, the bitter fighting of the Vietnam War spilled over into Laos. When the Vietnam War ended in 1975, the Pathet Lao set up a new communist republic in Laos. Today, the government of the country is strongly influenced by the policies of the Vietnamese communists.

FACTS AND FIGURES

Area: 91,428 sq. mi.
Population: 4,605,000
Capital: Vientiane (378,000)
Other major cities: Savannakhet (51,000), Pakse (45,000)
Highest point: Mt. Bia (9,250 ft.)
Official language: Lao
Main religions: Buddhism, traditional beliefs
Currency: Kip
Main exports: Timber, electricity, coffee, tin
Government: People's republic
Per capita GNP: U.S. $250

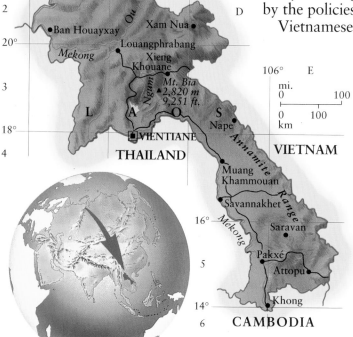

▼ Buddha Park lies about 12 miles (20 km) from the center of Vientiane. The grounds contain many Hindu, as well as Buddhist, sculptures. This site was built in the 1950s to honor both of these religions and their philosophies.

▼ A village woman carries baskets full of raw cotton. Cotton grows well in Laos's humid tropical climate and is one of the country's most important crops. Farmers either sell it or use it to make clothes for themselves.

▲ The small town and river port of Louangphrabang lies in the valley of the Mekong River. This region has an extremely dry climate. However, the land in the river valley is very fertile and crops such as rice and corn grow there. Louangphrabang has many Buddhist temples. One of these, on a hill called Phu Si , is said to have been built on the site of a footprint made by Buddha.

▼ Farmers pan for gold in the Mekong River. If they are lucky they will find a small amount of gold that they can sell for a little extra income.

477

VIETNAM

Most Vietnamese are rice farmers living in the deltas of the Red and the Mekong rivers. Here, and on the narrow coastal plain, the climate is hot and humid. It is cooler in the forested mountains inland, where bamboo and cinnamon are grown.

The French colonized Vietnam between the 1860s and 1880s. They developed rubber plantations and built factories in the cities. French rule ended in 1954, when communist guerrillas took over the north and the country was split into North Vietnam and South Vietnam. When communists tried to take over South Vietnam as well, North and South went to war. In 1965, the United States joined forces with the South against the communist North. The fighting got more intense and turned into a major war. The government of South Vietnam was overthrown in 1975. The U.S. troops left and the country became one again in 1976. Vietnam's economy suffered greatly as a result of the political isolation that the war caused. However, much has been done to repair the damage. Tourism has developed steadily, as has trade with countries such as Japan and Singapore.

◀ This stretch of beautiful coastline near Da Nang will soon be lined with hotels. Many are being built with U.S. money. Tourism is increasingly important, and Vietnam is aiming to attract around three million tourists each year.

478

FACTS AND FIGURES

Area: 127,241 sq. mi.
Population: 70,902,000
Capital: Hanoi
(1,089,000)
Other major city:
Ho Chi Minh City
(3,170,000)
Highest point:
Fan Si Pan (10,309 ft.)
Official language:
Vietnamese

Main religions: Taoism,
Buddhism, Christianity
Currency: Dong
Main exports: Coal,
agricultural products
including rice,
rubber, iron
Government: One-party
socialist republic
Per capita GNP:
Est. under U.S. $700

▼ *Farm workers wash carrots in the Mekong River. They wear traditional straw hats to shade themselves from the tropical sun.*

▲ *Followers of the Cao Dai religion celebrate mass in the Great Temple at Tay Ninh, southwest of An Loc. Their beliefs mix Islam, Christianity, Buddhism, and Taoism. Cao Dai has its own saints, including Joan of Arc from France and the British statesman Sir Winston Churchill.*

◀ *A Vietnamese army officer opens a trap door leading to underground tunnels. During the Vietnam War (1957–1975), the communists dug this maze of secret tunnels. Over 16,000 communists lived underground and attacked the U.S. troops from their hiding places.*

CHINA *Introduction*

China occupies about one-fifth of the Asian continent. This colossal country has the biggest population in the world—every day about 50,000 babies are born here. In order to provide food for such large numbers of people, every scrap of fertile land in the country has to be cultivated.

The river plains of eastern China have been farmed for thousands of years, and great industrial cities have grown up in this region. Fewer people live in the more remote regions of the north and west, which include barren deserts and high mountains.

China has one of the world's greatest and most ancient civilizations, with a written history that stretches back 3,500 years. Among its many inventions are paper, silk, and gunpowder.

In the course of this century China has experienced many changes. After more than 2,000 years as an empire, the country became a republic in 1911. Following an uprising in 1949, China became a communist state.

The 1990s saw a transformation in the major cities. Their narrow streets and low houses were replaced by freeways and high-rise buildings. By contrast, life has altered little in many rural areas for centuries. Most people are farmers and still use traditional methods to cultivate rice on the terraced rice paddies.

▼ *The Imperial Palace is one of many palaces in the Imperial City at the center of Beijing. In the days of the emperors, ordinary Chinese people were not allowed to step inside its high walls. This is why it became known as the Forbidden City. Today, many of the buildings are preserved as museums, which anyone can visit.*

◄ *A dragon is carried through the streets to the sound of exploding firecrackers during Chinese New Year celebrations . This festival is also celebrated in many overseas cities where people of Chinese descent have settled.*

ENDANGERED WORLD

The giant panda lives in the southwestern bamboo forests. Its future is threatened by the loss of this habitat and poaching.

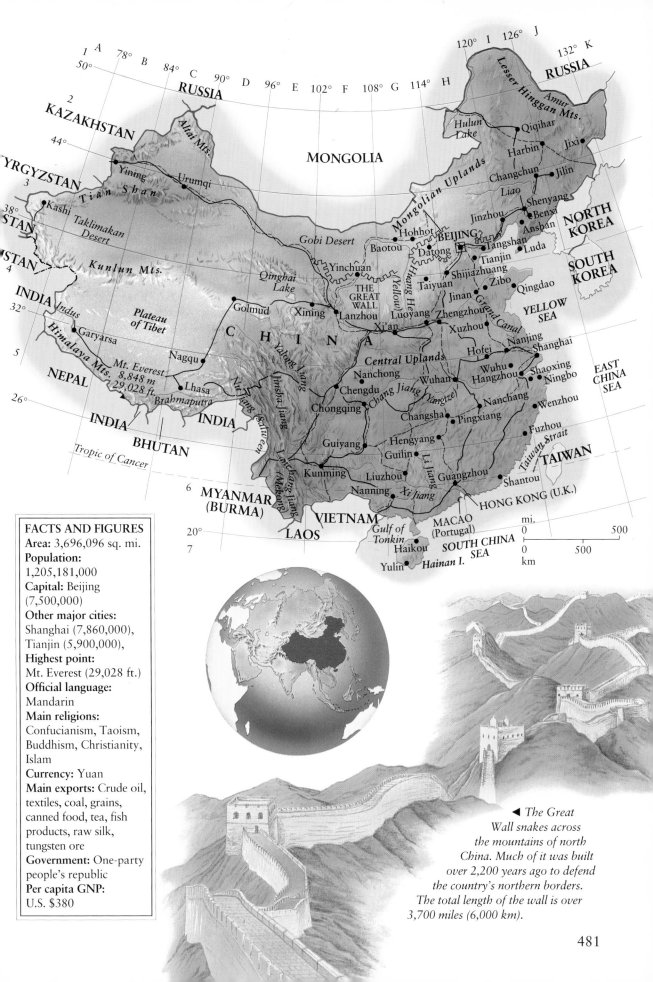

RUSSIA

KAZAKHSTAN

KYRGYZSTAN

TAN

STAN

INDIA

NEPAL

BHUTAN

INDIA

MONGOLIA

RUSSIA

Altai Mts.

Yining
Urumqi

Tian Shan

Kashi
Taklimakan
Desert

Kunlun Mts.

Plateau
of Tibet

Qinghai
Lake

Golmud

Xining

Gobi Desert

Baotou

Yinchuan

THE
GREAT
WALL

Lanzhou

Hohhot

Datong

Mongolian Uplands

Hulun
Lake

Qiqihar

Harbin

Jixi

Changchun

Jilin

Liao

Shenyang

Jinzhou

Benxi

Anshan

Tangshan

Tianjin

Luda

BEIJING

NORTH
KOREA

SOUTH
KOREA

Huang He

Hwang He
(Yellow)

Taiyuan

Shijiazhuang

Jinan

Zibo

Qingdao

YELLOW
SEA

Indus

Garyarsa

Himalaya Mts.

Mt. Everest
8,848 m
29,028 ft.

Nagqu

Lhasa

Brahmaputra

INDIA

Yalung Jiang

Yinsha Jiang

Nu Jiang (Salween)

Lancang Jiang (Mekong)

CHINA

Xi'an

Luoyang

Zhengzhou

Xuzhou

Grand Canal

Central Uplands

Nanchong

Chengdu

Chongqing

Wuhan

Chang Jiang (Yangtze)

Hofei

Nanjing

Shanghai

Wuhu

Hangzhou

Shaoxing

Ningbo

Nanchang

Wenzhou

Changsha

Pingxiang

Guiyang

Hengyang

Guilin

Li Jiang

Fuzhou

EAST
CHINA
SEA

Kunming

Liuzhou

Guangzhou

Shantou

Taiwan Strait

TAIWAN

Nanning

Xi Jiang

HONG KONG (U.K.)

MYANMAR
(BURMA)

VIETNAM

LAOS

Gulf of
Tonkin

MACAO
(Portugal)

Haikou

Yulin

Hainan I.

SOUTH CHINA
SEA

Tropic of Cancer

mi.
0   500
0   500
km

FACTS AND FIGURES

Area: 3,696,096 sq. mi.
Population:
1,205,181,000
Capital: Beijing
(7,500,000)
Other major cities:
Shanghai (7,860,000),
Tianjin (5,900,000),
Highest point:
Mt. Everest (29,028 ft.)
Official language:
Mandarin
Main religions:
Confucianism, Taoism,
Buddhism, Christianity,
Islam
Currency: Yuan
Main exports: Crude oil,
textiles, coal, grains,
canned food, tea, fish
products, raw silk,
tungsten ore
Government: One-party
people's republic
Per capita GNP:
U.S. $380

◀ The Great
Wall snakes across
the mountains of north
China. Much of it was built
over 2,200 years ago to defend
the country's northern borders.
The total length of the wall is over
3,700 miles (6,000 km).

CHINA *Geography*

China is the third largest country in the world after Canada and Russia. Its enormous landscape is full of contrasts, and the climate also varies from region to region. The far northeast has long, frozen winters and short, very hot summers. The land there is forested and rich in minerals, including coal. Extreme temperatures are also typical of the northern areas where grasslands border the wilderness of the Gobi Desert. In the summer the desert's daytime temperatures may be as high as 100°F (38°C), but they can fall to -29°F (-34°C) at night.

The central northern provinces are crossed by the Huang He (Yellow River). This broad, winding river is greatly feared for its terrible floods. However, rich mud from the same river has also made this a fertile farming region. Another waterway, the Chang Jiang (Yangtze River), cuts straight across the center of the country. It is China's most important trade route and the world's third longest river, flowing 3,900 miles (6,300 km) from the western mountains into the Yellow Sea.

China's western regions take in the high, bleak plateau of Tibet, which has often been called the "Roof of the World." To the south, the country is bordered by the Himalayan mountain range. The world's highest mountain, Mount Everest, is found there. The Himalayas descend into foothills in southwest China, where the climate is warm for much of the year. Both southern China and the nearby island of Hainan are hot and humid, with monsoon winds bringing heavy rain from May to October each year.

▼ *Yellow fields of rape plants brighten the rocky landscape near Xining. This is an arid region with harsh winters. The land here needs to be irrigated in order to give crops any chance of survival.*

▶ *The peaceful waters of Karakoli Lake may be seen from the Karakoram Highway, a rough road that carves its way through the remote mountains of the far west. The Karakoram Highway links China with northern Pakistan.*

ASIA

◀ *This Tibetan farming village lies on high ground, ringed by barren mountains. The summers here are short, but barley and vegetables can be grown before the winter sets in. Tibet is a remote region with an average of only five people per square mile (2.59 sq. km.).*

▶ *This village clings to a mountain peak in the Huangshan (Yellow Mountains), south of Wuhu. The misty summits, waterfalls, and forests in this area attract hikers from all over China.*

▼ *Pillars of limestone rock rise from the Li Jiang River at Yangshuo (Bright Moon), to the south of Guilin. This strange and beautiful landscape is a very popular destination for tourists.*

483

CHINA *Economy*

▼ *Trees are felled in snowy Heilongjiang, China's northernmost province. Logging is a key industry in China, and this province supplies timber to the rest of the nation. Heilongjiang also has reserves of oil, coal, iron ore, and gold.*

So many people live in China, and the country is so vast, that it could have one of the most powerful economies in the world. It has rich resources in the form of coal, oil, iron, tungsten, timber, hydroelectric power, and fisheries. Its fertile farmland could provide enough food for almost the whole population. China also has a centuries-old tradition of commerce, craft skills, and invention. It was Chinese scientists who brought the world the compass, fine porcelain, printing, and even paper money.

Despite all these advantages, the country has always had economic problems and still does today. Many of its minerals are found only in remote, inaccessible regions. There are large areas of barren wilderness where it is too dry to grow crops without irrigation. Also, expanding cities and factories have tended to spread across precious farmland. The people of China provide a large workforce, but as the population continues to grow, more resources are needed for food, health care, and education.

China's farmers and workers had suffered centuries of injustice and poverty when the communists came to power in 1949 and attempted to improve their lives. In the 1950s and 1960s, heavy industry was developed under state control. Farming was organized in units called communes, where villagers combined their land and farmed it together. From the 1980s, free markets, private ownership, and foreign investment were permitted. The economy boomed and Chinese goods were soon flooding into countries all over the world. Industrial modernization has continued and services such as up-to-date telecommunications networks have been developed.

▶ *Cotton is sorted at a village while ears of corn are laid out to dry in the sun. Before 1978, farming was organized by village groups called communes. Today, farming families have to provide a certain amount of crops for state organizations, but they can sell any extra produce at the local market.*

ECONOMIC SURVEY

Farming: China is the world leader in rice and tobacco. Barley, cotton, peanuts, corn, millet, tea, sorghum, and wheat are also grown in large quantities. More pigs are reared than in any other country. Cattle, sheep, goats, and camels are also kept.

Mining: Antimony, coal, iron ore, mercury, natural gas, oil, tin, and tungsten are produced.

Industry: Iron, steel, clothes, machinery, fertilizers, vehicles, ships, and toys are manufactured. Heavy industry has caused serious air and water pollution in some areas. Most industries are state-run, but foreign investment is now encouraged in special economic zones in the east of the country.

▶ Rice paddies are carved into the hillside around the southern city of Guiyang. Rice is China's most important crop and it is mostly grown south of the Chang Jiang (Yangtze River).

▶ A woman weaves an elaborate design in silk on a hand loom. Beautiful silk like this has been produced in China for thousands of years. In ancient times, the way in which silk thread was made from silkworms was a closely guarded secret.

◀ The iron and steel works in Baoshan, near the great port of Shanghai, is the most modern in China. It was completed in 1990 and produces high quality steel. China's steel industry is one of the largest and fastest growing in the world.

CHINA *People*

CHOW MEIN

Chow mein is a very popular main course in southern China. It consists of egg noodles that are stir-fried with vegetables and shredded chicken or other meat. The dish is flavored with sesame oil. Chinese cooking varies greatly from region to region, but noodles are eaten almost everywhere.

There have been many changes to Chinese life since the country became a communist state in 1949. The standard of living for most people has risen, especially for city dwellers. Family life, traditionally very important to the Chinese, has altered greatly. Several generations once lived in the same house, but families today are much smaller. Religious practices have also changed. For centuries religion was a central part of Chinese life, and many faiths existed side by side. When the communists came to power, however, religious belief was discouraged. This was especially true during the 1960s, a period known as the "Cultural Revolution." Today, the government is more tolerant and people are free to worship once more.

Like so many generations before them, more than three-fourths of all Chinese live in villages and farm the land. Wheat, corn, and rice are the main crops in the north, while rice and tea are important in the south. Chinese farmers currently produce enough food for the country's growing population. However, the government is worried that there will soon be too many people to feed. Laws have been passed to try to reduce the birth rate. People are not allowed to marry until they are in their early twenties, and couples are encouraged to have only one or two children.

Most people live in the crowded eastern part of the country where the land is suitable for growing crops. Over 90 percent of the population belongs to the Han group, who were originally a northern people. The rest is made up of over 50 other peoples including Mongols, Tibetans, Uygurs, Kazakhs, and Koreans.

◀ *Performers wear beautiful silk costumes and colorful makeup to star in a Beijing opera. This is China's most popular form of drama and includes traditional stories of princes, princesses, heroes, and villains. They are acted out with speech, songs, and dances, while musicians play offstage.*

◄ *People crowd a street in Shanghai, China's largest city. Scenes such as this are an everyday sight because of the huge population. Streets, apartment buildings, and public transportation are noisy and busy day and night.*

WUSHU

This girl is performing *wushu* one of the ancient Chinese martial arts. *Wushu* is a traditional form of exercise that develop both the mind and body. There are many different kinds of wushu, which may make use of bare hands, swords, or sticks. The most well-known form is *kung fu*.

SPEAK MANDARIN

Hello—你好
(*nee - how*)

Good-bye—再见
(*dzeh - jien*)

Please—请 (*ching*)

Thank you—谢谢
(*shay - shay*)

Yes—是 (*shi*)

No—不是 (*boo - shi*)

► *A Buddhist priest, or lama, chants from the scriptures during a funeral. The body is being cremated in the open air. Buddhism came to China from India before A.D. 100. Over the centuries it has played a very important part in Chinese history.*

CHINA *History*

About 9,000 years ago, Stone Age peoples were hunting and fishing along China's river valleys. By 5000 B.C., rice was cultivated here. Great civilizations developed from about 2100 B.C. In 221 B.C., Shi Huangdi, the first emperor of all China and founder of the Qin dynasty, came to the throne.

Defended to the north by its Great Wall, China soon ruled a vast empire with trading links as far away as ancient Rome. Despite wars during the Middle Ages, China also saw a golden age of the arts, technology, and exploration. The Mongols invaded China in the A.D. 1200s and brought a highly civilized way of life with them. Their leader Kublai Khan founded a new capital at Khanbalik (modern Beijing). The years of Mongol rule, known as the Yuan dynasty, were followed by the rule of the southern Chinese (the Ming) and by Manchus from the northeast (the Qing).

During the 1800s, China's power was challenged by European trading nations such as Britain. This led to wars and civil unrest inside China. In 1841, the Treaty of Nanking gave Britain the island of Hong Kong, which became a major trading port. (Hong Kong will return to Chinese rule in 1997.) During the early part of this century, the rule of the emperors collapsed. Years of chaos followed, marked by a power struggle between communists and nationalists, as well as an invasion by Japan. By 1948, the communists, under Mao Zedong, controlled the whole country. After Mao's death in 1976, China began to make economic reforms and increase trade with foreign countries.

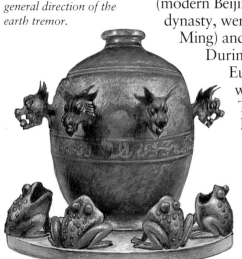

▼ *A Chinese scientist called Zhang Heng invented this seismograph (earthquake recorder) in A.D. 132. When an earthquake took place, a bronze ball would drop into the mouth of one of the frogs. This showed the general direction of the earth tremor.*

▶ *In 1989, students gathered in Beijing's Tiananmen Square demanding more freedom in China. This peaceful scene was soon shattered when troops fired into the crowd, killing hundreds of demonstrators. The protest movement was broken up, and many of its leaders fled abroad. The political system did not change.*

TAIWAN

FACTS AND FIGURES

Area: 13,969 sq. mi.
Population: 20,800,000
Capital: Taipei
(2,720,000)
Other major city:
Kaohsiung (1,400,000)
Highest point: Yu Shan
(13,110 ft.)
Official language:
Mandarin
Main religions: Taoism,
Buddhism
Currency:
New Taiwan dollar
Main exports: Electrical
equipment, machinery,
textiles, metal goods,
plastic goods
Government:
Multiparty republic
Per capita GNP:
Est. U.S. $10,200

The island of Taiwan is separated from mainland China by the narrow Formosa Strait. Formosa, which means "beautiful one," was the name given to Taiwan by Portuguese sailors in the 1500s.

Much of the island is mountainous and forested. There is lower ground in the west, where most people live. The moist, tropical climate enables farmers to grow crops such as rice and pineapples, although only about one-fourth of Taiwan can be farmed. Tuna, shrimp, and other fish are caught off the coast. Industry has become very important to the country's economy. Roughly one-third of Taiwan's workers now have jobs in manufacturing, and its factories export goods all over the world.

From the 1700s onward, the island was settled by China, but in 1895 it was taken over by Japan. Taiwan returned to Chinese rule in 1945 after the Japanese were defeated in World War II. In 1949, China became communist. The defeated leaders fled to Taiwan and set up a government there. Until 1971, anti-communist Taiwan represented all of China at the United Nations. Communist China then became internationally recognized. Taiwan lost its membership in the UN in 1971 and now it has official diplomatic ties with only a few countries. Tensions between Taiwan and China began to lessen during the early 1990s.

Map labels

B EAST CHINA 122° C
SEA
Formosa Strait
TAIPEI Chilung
Hsinchu
Suao 1
Tachia
Taichung
Changhua
Hualien 24°
TAIWAN
Chungyang Mts.
A 120°
Chiai
Tropic of Cancer
Pescadores
Yu Shan
3,997 m Yili
SOUTH Tainan 13,113 ft. PACIFIC
CHINA OCEAN
SEA
Kaohsiung Pingtung Taitung
mi.
0 50
0 50
km 22°
Oluan Pi

► Dragon dancers
celebrate Taiwan's Double
Tenth National Day, on
October 10 each year. It is
a national holiday and is
marked by huge parades
and firework displays.

MONGOLIA

▼ People celebrate May Day on the streets of the capital, Ulan Bator. Over one-fourth of the population live in this industrial town, which lies on the railroad line from Moscow, Russia, to Beijing, China.

The mountains, plateaus, and lakes of northern Mongolia give way to the Gobi Desert in the south, an empty wasteland of sand and gravel. Mongolia bakes in the summer and freezes under snow in the winter. By tradition, the Mongolians are herders. Mounted on stocky ponies, they cross these bleak landscapes in search of pasture for their sheep, cattle, and Bactrian camels. Today, encouraged by the government, many have settled to work on livestock farms. Others have jobs in factories or mining.

In the Middle Ages, Mongolia built one of the largest empires the world has ever seen. Under their leader, Genghis Khan, Mongolian horsemen conquered land from central Europe to the Far East. This empire soon fragmented, and Mongolia was swallowed up by China. In 1924, most of it became a communist republic that was strongly influenced by the Soviet Union. The communists took property away from the country's noble families and destroyed Buddhist monasteries. They also began to develop industry. With the collapse of the Soviet Union in 1991, Mongolia developed as a multiparty democracy. It faced economic problems without Soviet support. At the same time, many Mongolians took new pride in their history and religious traditions, which had been suppressed since the 1920s.

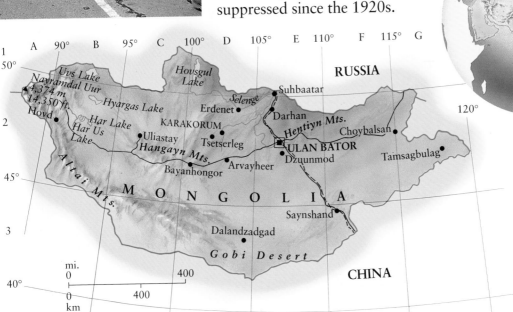

◄ Wrapped up warmly against the bitter winds, a Mongolian woman brings in the hay with a horse-drawn cart. The carts behind are hauled by Bactrian (two-humped) camels. Beyond the fields stretch the bare hills of this sparsely populated country. Very little land in Mongolia is suitable for cultivation. Even so, the government is encouraging farmers to grow grain, potatoes, and vegetables to reduce imports of food.

FACTS AND FIGURES
Area: 604,826 sq. mi.
Population: 2,371,000
Capital: Ulan Bator (575,000)
Other major cities: Darhan (87,000), Erdenet (59,000)
Highest point: Nayramdal Uur (14,347 ft.)
Official language: Mongolian
Main religion: Buddhism
Currency: Tugrik
Main exports: Minerals, fuels, food, consumer goods, nonfood raw materials
Government: Multiparty republic
Per capita GNP: Est. U.S. $700–3,000

▶ In some areas of Mongolia people live in traditional gers. These round tents have a frame of wooden slats covered with thick felt. Some gers are set up permanently outside towns to solve local housing shortages.

◄ Horse racing is popular throughout Mongolia. Boys and girls as young as five take part in races all over the country. There are large prizes of cash, silk cloth, or household goods. Jockeys usually retire around the age of 12.

NORTH KOREA

North Korea is a communist country where all the factories, farms, and even the cars, are owned by the government. The farms are collectives, which means that work and profits are shared. Until the 1950s, most North Koreans worked as farmers, but today more than half the country's workers have jobs in factories. Most of them cycle to work, leaving their babies in state-run nurseries.

North Korea and South Korea formed a single country for hundreds of years, from the 1300s until this century. Between 1910 and 1945, Korea was occupied by Japan. This ended when Japan was defeated in World War II. After this, the country was divided in two, with troops from the Soviet Union occupying northern Korea and United States troops occupying the south. In 1950, North Korea, backed by the Soviet Union and China, attacked South Korea, which was supported by the United States. Millions were killed or made homeless. The war ended in 1953, but tension between North and South Korea continued, despite peace talks from the 1970s onward. Under communist rule, reunification with South Korea still appears unlikely in the short term.

◀ There are many statues of heroic communist workers in North Korea. Since the country became communist in 1948, it has become heavily industrialized.

FACTS AND FIGURES

Area: 47,398 sq. mi.
Population: 23,054,000
Capital: Pyongyang (2,640,000)
Other major cities: Hamhung (775,000), Chongjin (755,000)
Highest point: Paektu Mt. (9,000 ft.)
Official language: Korean
Main religions: Traditional beliefs, Ch'ondogyo (combines elements of Roman Catholicism, Buddhism, Confucianism, Taoism, and shamanism)
Currency: Won
Main exports: Coal, iron, copper, textiles
Government: Single-party republic
Per capita GNP: Est. U.S. $700–3,000

SOUTH KOREA

FACTS AND FIGURES

Area: 38,330 sq. mi.
Population: 44,056,000
Capital: Seoul
(10,628,000)
Other major cities:
Pusan (3,798,000),
Taegu (2,229,000),
Inchon(1,819,000)
Highest point:
Halla Mt. (6,396 ft.)
**Official
language:**
Korean
Main religions:
Buddhism,
Christianity
Currency: Won
Main exports:
Machinery, transporta-
tion equipment,
manufactured products
Government:
Multiparty republic
Per capita GNP:
U.S. $6,790

South Korea has one of the world's fastest-growing economies. Its industry is highly developed, with factories producing computers, electrical goods, optical equipment, and heavy machinery. The country's rapid industrial growth has taken place since the 1950s. Before this, its economy was largely based on agriculture. Unlike North Korea, South Korea is not a communist country and most of its industry is privately owned.

In the south and west of South Korea cool, forested mountains descend to a fertile plain. Farmers grow rice in these humid coastal regions and fish are caught in the Yellow Sea.

South and North Korea were once a single country, but divided in 1945. After World War II, the United States took control of South Korea, while the Soviet Union held North Korea. From 1950 to 1953, war raged between the two. Since then, South Korea has seen political turmoil and harsh military rule. However, during the late 1980s, it began to move toward a more democratic system. It became a multiparty republic and held democratic elections.

► *This palace in Seoul was the center of the Choson Kingdom. Korea (North and South) was called Choson from 1392 until 1910, when it was invaded by Japan.*

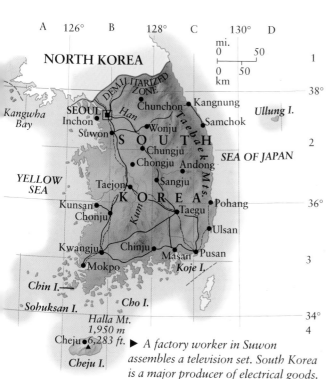

► *A factory worker in Suwon assembles a television set. South Korea is a major producer of electrical goods.*

JAPAN *Introduction*

The Japanese call their island country Nippon, meaning "the source of the sun." This ancient name explains the red disc on their national flag, which represents the rising sun.

For many centuries emperors have been heads of state in Japan. Until the 1900s, Japanese emperors claimed to be divine, believing they were descended from the gods. The amount of power held by the emperor has varied greatly from one era to another. Today, the emperor's role and duties are ceremonial only. The government of the nation is carried out by a democratic parliament called the Diet.

The Diet is made up of an elected House of Representatives and a House of Councillors. Political parties include socialists, liberals, and communists, but since 1955, the most successful party has been the conservative Liberal Democratic Party.

Modern Japan is world-famous for its powerful business corporations and advanced electronic technology. However, this is still a land in which traditions and ancient customs are held in the highest respect. Among the busy streets and bright lights of the capital, visitors can glimpse the past in the form of temples and shrines. They can also take part in *chanoyu*, a 500-year-old tea-drinking ceremony that honors courtesy and hospitality.

Most of the population live in crowded cities on the coastal plains. Farther inland, much of the country is covered with forested hills and mountains. The land is both beautiful and unstable—there are many volcanoes, and earthquakes are common throughout Japan.

FACTS AND FIGURES
Area: 145,840 sq. mi.
Population: 124,959,000
Capital: Tokyo (7,976,000)
Other major cities: Yokohama (3,233,000), Osaka (2,506,000), Nagoya (2,098,000)
Highest point: Mt. Fuji (12,385 ft.)
Official language: Japanese
Main religions: Shintoism, Buddhism
Currency: Yen
Main exports: Machinery, vehicles, ships, electronic equipment, steel, chemicals, textiles
Government: Constitutional monarchy
Per capita GNP: U.S. $28,220

ENDANGERED WORLD

Hunting of the red-crowned Manchurian crane led to its near-extinction. Now it is protected.

▶ *The active volcano Sakurajima towers behind the modern city of Kagoshima. Over half a million people live in this seaport, which is on the southern island of Kyushu. It is famous for its textiles and pottery.*

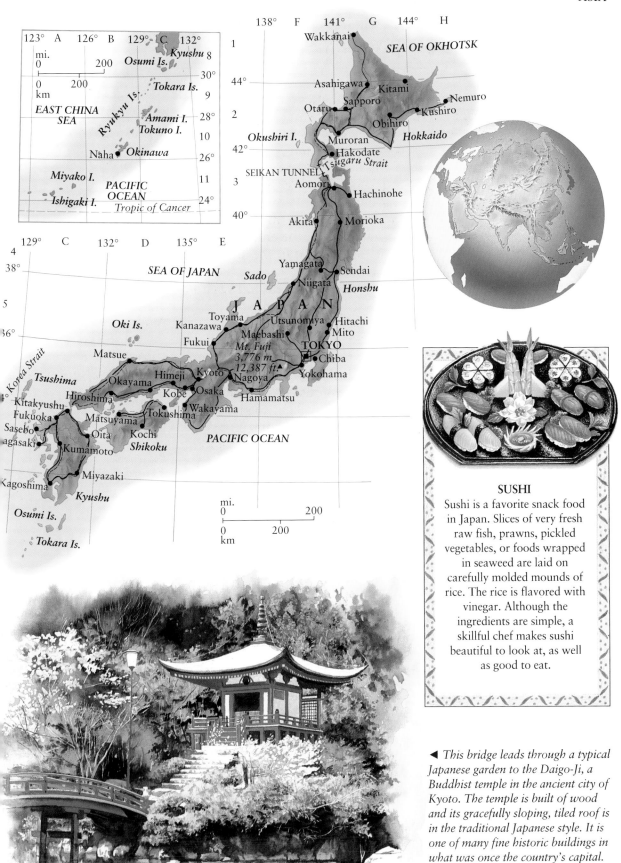

SUSHI

Sushi is a favorite snack food in Japan. Slices of very fresh raw fish, prawns, pickled vegetables, or foods wrapped in seaweed are laid on carefully molded mounds of rice. The rice is flavored with vinegar. Although the ingredients are simple, a skillful chef makes sushi beautiful to look at, as well as good to eat.

◄ This bridge leads through a typical Japanese garden to the Daigo-Ji, a Buddhist temple in the ancient city of Kyoto. The temple is built of wood and its gracefully sloping, tiled roof is in the traditional Japanese style. It is one of many fine historic buildings in what was once the country's capital.

JAPAN *Geography*

▼ *Steam rises from hot springs at Beppu, near Oita on Kyushu. The waters are heated deep inside the volcanic rocks below. Hot springs are found all over Japan.*

Japan is made up of about 3,000 islands, which form a long chain off the eastern coast of Asia. The biggest islands are Honshu, Hokkaido, Shikoku, and Kyushu. Most Japanese live on these four islands, even though much of the land is taken up by towering mountains and hills covered in forest. Streams and waterfalls tumble down the steep slopes in this spectacular landscape.

Farming is difficult everywhere except on the narrow coastal lowlands. These include some of the most crowded regions on Earth, with cities such as Tokyo and Yokohama forming huge urban areas. To help satisfy the need for more land, parts of the coastline have been reclaimed from the sea.

The islands are the tops of a huge mountain range that rises from the floor of the Pacific Ocean. This is a weak area of the Earth's crust, and its rocks are still on the move. Volcanoes and earth tremors are common in Japan and major earthquakes have caused devastation throughout its history. Sometimes an earthquake sets off a huge wave called a *tsunami*. These waves have flooded coastal areas and sunk ships.

A journey from north to south takes in a variety of climates. In the north, there are cool summers and cold, snowy winters. Moving south, winters become milder and summers warm and humid. The Ryukyu islands have a tropical climate. Fall and spring are bright and sunny in much of Japan, and in spring the countryside is filled with cherry and plum blossoms.

▶ *Surveyors check earthquake damage to measure how far the rocks have shifted. A terrible earthquake destroyed Tokyo in 1923. During the massive earthquake of 1995, thousands died in the rubble of Japan's fifth largest city, Kobe.*

◀ A family clears a path through a high snowdrift. Hokkaido and the northwestern part of Honshu receive heavy snowfalls in winter when bitter winds blow in from northern Russia across the Sea of Japan. Snow can last for more than six months in some areas.

▼ The snowcapped slopes of Mount Fuji look so peaceful that it is hard to believe this is a volcano. It last erupted in 1707. Japan's highest mountain has inspired artists for centuries. Its many shrines and temples are visited by pilgrims.

▶ Rocky headlands and stacks (pillars of rock) extend from the Oki Islands into the Sea of Japan. The Okis lie off the coast of Honshu, north of the town of Matsue. Air and sea routes link these islands to mainland Honshu.

JAPAN *Economy*

▼ *Harvested rice is stacked for drying and threshing, as it has been for thousands of years. Modern machinery is now used to do jobs like this on many farms. Rice is the most important food in Japan and is eaten with almost every meal.*

Japan is a land of economic miracles. One miracle is the way in which land is used. Modern farming methods make it possible for the very small amount of land suitable for farming to produce large crops of rice, tea, potatoes, fruit, rapeseed, and tobacco. These methods include growing specially developed strains of crops that give high yields and using fertilizers and pesticides. Modern equipment, such as specialized rice-planting machines, also means that far fewer people are needed to work the land.

Another miracle is how these small islands have become one of the world's greatest industrial powers. They have achieved this with hard work and investment in new technology. Japan has to import huge amounts of oil and raw materials for industry, but it produces more cars and color televisions than any other country. Japanese firms have opened factories all over the world. However, they do face increasing competition from other Asian countries such as South Korea.

Some people believe that Japan is so successful because the working conditions here promote hard work. Large companies often demand great loyalty from their staff. Employees may be expected to sing a special company song, wear the company uniform, and join in physical exercise sessions each day. In return, many employers organize their workers' vacations, health care, and housing.

▶ *A farm worker drives a machine that sprays fruit trees with pesticides. This will help to produce a larger fruit crop. Japanese farms use modern technology to grow a large amount of food on a small area of land.*

◄ *These modern offices in Tokyo's Ginza district are typical of the city's many business buildings. Tokyo is the center of the Japanese business world. It also has one of the world's leading stock exchanges. Twenty-six percent of the Japanese labor force work in finance and commerce.*

ECONOMIC SURVEY

Farming: Japanese farmers produce much of the nation's food, despite the shortage of farmland. About half the usable land is given over to rice. Fruit and vegetables are also grown. Dairy production is increasing.

Fishing: Japan, with China and Russia, is one of the leading fishing nations. It accounts for about one-tenth of the world catch.

Mining: Japan has only a small quantity of minerals. It has to import most raw materials and fuel.

Industry: Manufactured goods include electronic products, cameras, watches, machinery, cars, ships, silk and other textiles, plastics, and ceramics. It is also a major producer of steel and chemicals.

▲ *Automated robotic machinery saves time and money on the car production line. Japanese firms were among the first to introduce modern methods of assembling vehicles. Manufacturers such as Toyota and Honda are famous all over the world.*

► *Octopuses are sold at the Tokyo fish market. Japan is one of the world's leading fishing nations and fish is an important part of the Japanese diet. Large catches include mackerel, herring, and tuna.*

JAPAN *People*

The first inhabitants of Japan may have been the Ainu, a pale-skinned people. Their descendants now live on Hokkaido and a few of Japan's northern islands. Some Ainu villages survive, but many Ainu have intermarried with the Japanese. Most of today's Japanese are descended from peoples who migrated to the country from the Asian mainland thousands of years ago. Minority groups include Koreans and Chinese.

Today, the majority of Japanese live in the crowded cities on Honshu island. They may work in offices, banks, factories, or department stores and usually travel to work by train.

Before 1945, most Japanese lived in rural villages. Families were large, with several generations often sharing the same household. Now smaller families are common, and many city people live in small apartments. However, the old way of life has not entirely disappeared. There are still traditional Japanese houses with sliding screens and floor mats called tatami. Also, the traditional silk robe, or kimono, is still worn by men and women on special occasions.

Complicated gadgets, arcade games, computers, and television are all a vital part of life in modern Japan, but there is a very different side to the Japanese. For centuries this has shown itself in the simple beauty of Japanese architecture, gardens, art, and ceramics. A love of nature is also important. This is reflected in the ancient religion of Shinto and in Japanese forms of Buddhism. Followers of Shinto, for example, worship the spirits of trees, rocks, mountains, rivers, and other forces of nature.

▼ *Decorated boats take to the sea during a festival at Shiogama, northeast of Sendai. They are followed out by the local fishing fleet. Every summer the boats sail to a nearby island, where they give thanks for their catch.*

▼ *These girls are practicing a custom called* nagashi-bina. *This takes place during the Shinto festival,* Hinamatsuri. *Paper dolls or flowers are floated down a river, and this is believed to take away a person's troubles.*

KENDO
Kendo students attempt to score points by striking their opponent in a ritual contest. Kendo is a martial art that aims to develop self-control. It is a form of fencing that uses long bamboo staves instead of swords. The fighters wear long black skirts, padded gloves, light armor, and helmets. Kendo has its origins in the training of the samurai, the warriors of ancient Japan. The modern form was developed in the late 1700s.

▼ The temple of the Golden Pavilion is one of the most famous buildings in Japan and stands amid beautiful, landscaped gardens in the historic city of Kyoto. It was built in 1394 as a Buddhist temple. Today, it contains a rich collection of art treasures and is more of a tourist attraction than a place of worship. Buddhism is the main religion in Japan with more than 90 million followers.

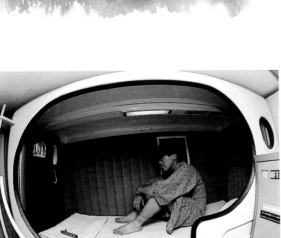

▲ This tiny sleeping space is a room in a Japanese invention called a capsule hotel. The sleeping capsules were designed to save space and are cheaper than rooms in ordinary city center hotels. They are often used by business people on short city visits.

SPEAK JAPANESE

Hello—こんにちは
(kon - nich - ee - wah)

Good-bye—さようなら
(sah - yoh - nah - rah)

Please—どうぞ
(doh - zoh)

Thank you—ありがとう
(a - ree - gah - toh)

JAPAN *History*

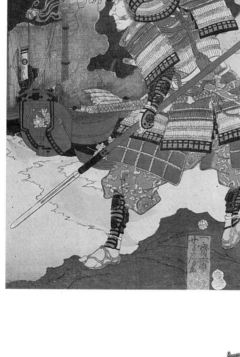

▼ *A famous samurai (warrior) of the 1300s, named Shirafuji Hikoshichiro, watches enemy ships burning. Japanese samurai wore elaborate armor and helmets and carried some of the deadliest swords ever made. This picture, by Utagawa Kuniyoshi, was painted in about 1840.*

Little is known about the early history of Japan. Ancient Japanese chronicles and legends state that the first emperor, Jimmu Tenno, ruled from 660 B.C. Scientists believe that people have lived on the Japanese islands since at least 4500 B.C. and that by 200 B.C. there were settled farming communities here. In about A.D. 550, Buddhism arrived in Japan when the king of Pakche in southwest Korea sent Buddhist priests over to the country.

The Middle Ages was a time of turmoil. Power passed from the emperors to warlords called shoguns. Sometimes there were civil wars between rival bands of warriors called samurai. In 1603, Tokugawa Ieyasu became shogun of a united Japan. By this time Portuguese traders and Christian priests had arrived, but Ieyasu expelled them. After this, Japan closed its doors to the outside world until the 1850s. In 1867, the ruling shogun was overthrown, and power returned to the royal family with Mutsuhito as emperor. A period of rapid industrialization followed.

During the 1930s, the Japanese army invaded China. Then, during World War II, it overran most of Southeast Asia and the Pacific Islands. Japan was defeated in World War II and occupied by United States forces until 1952. Since the 1950s, the war-damaged economy has grown rapidly and today Japan is a major world economic power.

▶ *Himeji castle was one of many splendid buildings erected by the samurai general Toyotomi Hideyoshi (1536–1598). Hideyoshi was the son of a humble woodcutter, but he rose to fame as a ruthless warrior. For the last ten years of his life, he was the most powerful man in Japan.*

502

◀ *Actors wearing traditional costume and makeup perform a Japanese kabuki play. Kabuki is a type of drama that was developed during the late 1600s. It is still performed in Japan today. Men play female roles as well as male parts and act out exciting historical stories to the sound of music and singing. Japanese forms of drama have existed for centuries, and in modern times they have had an important influence on world theater.*

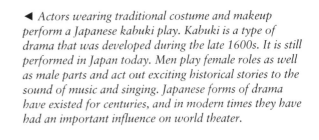

COMMODORE PERRY

On March 31, 1854, Commodore Matthew Perry, commander of a U.S. squadron, signed a treaty with the Japanese emperor. As a result, Japanese ports were opened to Western traders for the first time in over 200 years. Many Japanese people disapproved of Western influences, but in 1868, the emperor decided to modernize Japan. Western ideas and technology were rapidly introduced. By the 1900s, Japan had become a major world power.

◀ *This children's memorial stands in the Peace Park in Hiroshima. World War II ended in 1945 when the United States dropped atomic bombs on Hiroshima and Nagasaki. Both cities were utterly destroyed. Over 155,000 civilians were killed in Hiroshima alone.*

SINGAPORE

▲ Singapore City is a busy port built on the south coast of the largest island. More than 90 percent of the population live in this crowded city of towering apartment buildings and gleaming high-rise offices.

Over 50 islands make up the Republic of Singapore. The largest is linked by road across the Johor Strait to mainland Malaysia. Many of the smaller islands are uninhabited. Singapore lies just above the equator, so the climate is hot and sticky. It is a country that cannot produce enough food for its own population, and water supplies have to be piped in from Malaysia. Yet Singapore has become one of the richest countries in Southeast Asia. Almost all its rain forest has been cut down to make room for homes, businesses, or parks and there is very little agricultural land. The country's wealth is based on shipping, banking, electronics manufacture, and international trade.

There is a legend that Singapore was founded by a Malay prince who landed on the island in 1299. Over the centuries many Chinese people have settled here to work and trade. Modern Singapore was founded in 1819 by Sir Stamford Raffles, who was a trader with the British East India Company. Britain ruled the country from 1858 until 1959. In 1963, Singapore became part of the Federation of Malaysia, but it withdrew to become a separate nation in 1965. The people live under very strict laws. Any religion can be practiced, but gambling and even chewing gum are forbidden. There are also huge fines for dropping litter. Personal freedom is limited, but the crime rate is the lowest in the world.

FACTS AND FIGURES

Area: 247 sq. mi.
Population: 2,874,000
Capital: Singapore City
Highest point: Timah Hill (580 ft.)
Official languages: English, Mandarin, Malay, Tamil
Main religions: Buddhism, Taoism, Islam, Christianity, Hinduism
Currency: Singaporean dollar
Main exports: Machinery, vehicles, electronic equipment, petroleum products, rubber, chemicals, food, clothes
Government: Multiparty republic
Per capita GNP: U.S. $15,750

MAJULAH SINGAPURA

Brunei

Singapore

A 103°40'   B   103°50'   C   104° D

MALAYSIA

1

Johor Strait

Kranji   Nee Soon   Sembawang   Punggol   Tekong Besar I.
1°25'   Seletar   Ubin I.

Bukit Panjang   Timah Hill   Serangoon Harbour   Changi
Choa Chu Kang   177 m 581 ft.

S I N G A P O R E   Singapore Strait
2   Jurong   Bukit   Paya Lebar
Tuas   Timah Village   Bedok

Ayer Chawan I.   Ayer Merbau I.   ■ SINGAPORE CITY
1°15'   Keppel Harbour
Bukum I.   Sentosa I.   mi.
3   0   5
Pawai I.   Semakau I.   0   5
Senang I.   km

BRUNEI

The Sultan of Brunei is the richest ruler in the world. His small nation on the north coast of the island of Borneo has become vastly wealthy since oil was discovered there in the 1920s. Reserves of oil and natural gas are now beginning to run low, so the government is encouraging development of banana and rubber plantations as well as other private businesses.

Seventy percent of the mostly Malay and Chinese population live in cities. Over half work for the government, some in the state-owned oil industry. Education and health care are paid for by the government from oil profits, and the standard of living is high. Even those who choose to live in traditional longhouses (wooden buildings that house dozens of families) often own luxury cars. Others live in water villages called *kampongs*, where houses are built on stilts and boats ferry people around.

Brunei once ruled a large area of Borneo, but over the centuries its power was weakened by piracy and lawlessness. From the 1800s, it was a protectorate of Britain, so Britain looked after its foreign affairs and defense in return for shipping rights. Brunei received full independence from Britain in 1984.

▲ *Children celebrate Brunei's Independence Day by parading in colorful costumes and waving butterfly wands or paper flowers. Flag-waving crowds gather near the royal palace to greet the sultan (king and ruler).*

FACTS AND FIGURES

Area: 2,226 sq. mi.
Population: 276,000
Capital: Bandar Seri Begawan (46,000)
Other major city: Seria (21,000)
Highest point: Pagon (6,068 ft.)
Official language: Malay
Main religions: Islam, Buddhism, Christianity
Currency: Bruneian dollar (ringgit)
Main exports: Crude oil, liquefied natural gas, petroleum products
Government: Absolute monarchy
Per capita GNP: Est. over U.S. $8,000

▶ *The Belait River winds through dense green tropical rain forest. Three-fourths of Brunei is forested and home to brilliantly colored butterflies, flying squirrels, hornbills, monkeys, wild pigs, and deer.*

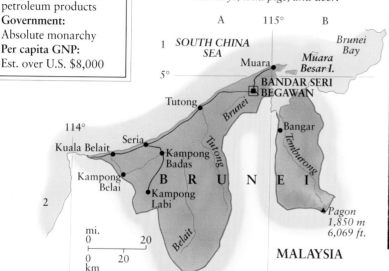

PHILIPPINES

The Philippines is a nation of more than 7,000 islands. The larger islands are mountainous, with over 30 active volcanoes. Much of the land is clad in forest where bamboo, orchids, and a huge variety of trees grow. Unfortunately, the country's rich resources have been ruthlessly plundered. Logging companies have felled millions of hardwood trees, causing problems with soil erosion.

About half the population earn their living by farming, growing rice, sugarcane, pineapples, bananas, and coconuts. The economy is based mainly on agriculture and timber production. However, the manufacturing industry is expanding, producing clothing and processed foods. Fishing provides much of the islanders' food.

The Filipinos are descended from Malays who arrived around 3000 B.C. Spain colonized the islands in 1565 and named them after its king, Philip II. After the Spanish-American War of 1898, the United States bought the Philippines for 20 million dollars. Independence came in 1946, and under the dictatorship of President Marcos the islands experienced censorship, corruption, and poverty. Many left to work abroad. Marcos was overthrown in 1986 and fled to the United States. Today's government is working to solve the environmental and economic problems that he left behind.

▼ *The rice terraces at Banawe in northern Luzon were dug out 2,000 years ago. Channels and pipes bring water to the seedlings. In the 1960s, an organization based in the Philippines developed a new rice plant to double the grain yield. This has increased rice production, but the fertility of much of the land has been ruined by the new pesticides used.*

◀ *Workers make wicker furniture in a rattan factory. Masks are worn to protect them against the dust and splinters. Rattan is a cane that is taken from the stem of the rattan palm, a type of climbing plant. This palm is common throughout Southeast Asia. Because it is strong, flexible, and long-lasting, rattan is ideal for a wide range of uses, from baskets to ships' cables.*

A 118° B 120° C 122° D 124° E 126° F

Batan Is.

Babuyan Is.

Laoag Aparri

Cordillera Central

Tuguegarao

Baguio City

Luzon

Tarlac Cabanatuan

Angeles

MANILA Quezon City

Daet

Batangas

SOUTH CHINA SEA

Calapan Naga

Mindoro *Catanduanes I.*

Sorsogon

Calamian Group

Masbate

Masbate

Panay Catbalogan

P H I L I P P I N E S *Samar*

Tacloban

Iloilo *Cebu* *Leyte*

Bacolod Cebu City *PHILIPPINE SEA*

Puerto Princesa *Negros* *Bohol* Surigao

Dumaguete Tagbilaran

Palawan Dipolog Butuan

Cagayan de Oro

SULU SEA Malaybalay

Pagadian Davao

Zamboanga Mt. Apo
2,954 m
9,690 ft.

Mindanao

Jolo General Santos

Sulu Archipelago *CELEBES SEA*

mi.
0 200
0 200
km

FACTS AND FIGURES
Area: 115,830 sq. mi.
Population: 65,649,000
Capital: Manila
(1,599,000)
Other major cities:
Quezon City
(1,667,000);
Davao (850,000)
Highest point:
Mt. Apo (9,689 ft.)
Official languages:
Filipino, English
Main religions:
Christianity, Islam
Currency:
Philippino peso
Main exports: Clothes,
electronic equipment,
coconut oil, timber
Government:
Multiparty republic
Per capita GNP:
U.S. $770

▼ *The streets of Manila are crowded with jeepneys. These are jeeps fitted with a long bus body, which is painted and decorated in bright colors. The jeepneys are used for public transportation.*

SPEAK FILIPINO

Hello—Kumusta
(*koo - moos - tah*)

Good-bye—Paalam
(*pah - ah - lahm*)

Please—Paki (*par - kee*)

Thank you—Salamat
(*sah - lah - maht*)

Yes— Oo (*o'o*)

No—Hindi (*hin - day*)

MALAYSIA

Malaysia is a green land with mountains cloaked in rain forest, huge plantations of rubber and oil palms, and sandy beaches. A thousand different orchids bloom in the tropical forests, which are home to many wild animals and plants. Wildlife such as tigers, leopards, and rhinoceroses are protected in several national parks.

Many Malays live in farm villages strung out along the roads between rice paddies and pineapple fields. Along the coast most people fish for a living. A large Chinese minority (35 percent of the population) lives mainly in the cities. This is an Islamic country, but all kinds of religions are practiced here. Malaysia is dotted with Buddhist and Taoist temples as well as Christian churches.

The ancestors of today's Malays came from China around 2000 B.C. Many made their living by fishing or piracy along the swampy coast of Sarawak. The Arabs, Portuguese, and Dutch all occupied this area before the British seized control in the early 1800s. After the Japanese occupation during World War II, communist guerrillas launched a terrorist campaign against the British. Independence came to peninsular Malaysia in 1957, and by 1963, the eastern territories had joined the new nation.

Malaysia has a democratic system of government. Since independence it has achieved economic success with rubber, tin, and oil. Timber-felling has laid waste great areas of forest but is now controlled by the government.

CHICKEN SATAY
Small pieces of chicken or other meat are skewered and barbecued over glowing charcoal to make satay. The dish is flavored with spices and served with a hot peanut sauce. It is often eaten with sliced cucumbers, onions, and *ketupat* (boiled rice wrapped in palm leaves).

▼ *In the capital, Kuala Lumpur, modern architecture contrasts with the traditional Islamic style of the government buildings. This city is the center of business and industry.*

SPEAK MALAYSIAN

Good-bye—Selamat tinggal
(*se - lah - mat **tin** – gahl*)

Please—Tolong (**toh** - *long*)

Thank you—Terima kasih
(*te - ree - mah **kah** – see*)

Yes—Ya (*yah*)

No—Tidak (*tee - **dak***)

◀ *Tea is grown in the Cameron Highlands, to the east of Ipoh. This cool hill country is surrounded by green mountains and sparkling waterfalls. The fertile soil supports fine fruit, vegetables, and flowers, which are grown in large market gardens.*

FACTS AND FIGURES

Area: 127,250 sq. mi.
Population: 19,239,000
Capital: Kuala Lumpur (938,000)
Other major cities: Ipoh (301,000), George Town (251,000) Johor Bahru (250,000)
Highest point: Mt. Kinabalu (13,428 ft.)
Official language: Bahasa Malaysia
Main religions: Islam, Buddhism
Currency: Malaysian dollar (ringgit)
Main exports: Rubber, palm oil, timber, petroleum, tin, electronic equipment
Government: Federal constitutional monarchy
Per capita GNP: U.S. $2,790

▶ *A man practices kite-flying. This sport is a popular pastime among villagers in the east of the country. Competitions are held to see whose kite can fly the highest or stay in the air for the longest time.*

509

INDESIA *Introduction*

Indonesia is the world's biggest archipelago—a long chain of more than 13,600 mountainous islands. Their many active volcanoes form part of the danger zone that geologists call the "Pacific Ring of Fire." Indonesia has seen some of the most violent volcanic eruptions ever recorded. However, people continue to live close to the smoldering volcanoes because their ash makes the soil rich and fertile.

The islands are watered by monsoon rains and warmed by humid tropical heat. There are clear lakes, coastal mangrove swamps, and some of the most spectacular rain forests on Earth. Rafflesia, the world's largest flower, blooms here. This bright orange flower is up to three feet (one m) across, with a nasty stench that attracts insects. Many rare animals, such as tigers and rhinoceroses, roam through the forests, but logging companies are destroying their habitat to fell precious hardwoods such as teak and ebony.

The economy is based on agriculture, forestry, and fishing. Indonesia has one of the world's largest fishing industries. Its seas yield plentiful supplies of mackerel, anchovies, and tuna, as well as pearls and shells. Spices such as pepper, cloves, and nutmeg once made this country an important destination for traders and pirates, and they are still grown today. Other products include rubber, coffee, tobacco, and petroleum. The country's mines yield copper, nickel, and coal. Reserves of oil have been exploited since the 1960s, and income from this has helped to boost the economy.

▼ *Men on the island of Bali perform the Hindu temple ceremony known as Kecak. The word* kecak *means monkey. The men fall into a trance in which they believe they are possessed by the spirits of monkeys. This island is famous for its Hindu ceremonies and festivals.*

◄ *These distinctive wooden houses have curved roofs with tall gable ends that make them look like boats. The houses are built on stilts and are entered by carved steps and beautifully decorated doorways. They are the homes of the Toraja peoples, who live in central Sulawesi.*

| | 95° A | 100° B | 105° C | 110° D | 115° E | 120° F | 125° G | 130° H | 135° I | 140° J |

SOUTH CHINA SEA

mi.
0   500
0   500
km

Banda Aceh

MALAYSIA
SINGAPORE
Medan
Pekanbaru
Padang
Palembang
Bengkulu
Telukbetung
Bandung
Yogyakarta

Natuna Besar Is.
BRUNEI
MALAYSIA

Borneo
Pontianak
Banjarmasin

Sumatra
Bangka I.
Belitung I.
JAKARTA
Semarang
Surabaya
Lombok I.
Sumbawa I.
Bali
Sumba I.

Mentawai Is.
Barisan Mts.

INDIAN OCEAN

Java
Malang
Madura I.

CELEBES SEA
Manado
Palu
Balikpapan
Sulawesi
Parepare
Ujungpandang

MOLUCCA SEA
Sula Is.
Buru I.
Butung I.

Talaud Is.
Sangihe Is.
Morotai I.
Halmahera I.

Doberai Peninsula
Misool I.
Ceram
Kai Is.

Biak I.
Jayapura

PACIFIC OCEAN
Equator

PAPUA NEW GUINEA

Puncak Jaya
5,030 m
16,503 ft.

Aru Is.
New Guinea

INDONESIA

BANDA SEA
Wetar I.
Tanimbar Is.

JAVA SEA
FLORES SEA
Flores I.
Timor
Dili
Kupang

ARAFURA SEA

FACTS AND FIGURES

Area: 741,097 sq. mi.
Population: 189,136,000
Capital: Jakarta (6,504,000)
Other major city: Surabaya (2,028,000)
Highest point: Puncak Jaya (16,498 ft.)
Official language: Bahasa Indonesia
Main religions: Islam, Christianity, Hinduism, Buddhism
Currency: Rupiah
Main exports: Oil, liquefied natural gas, timber, rubber coffee
Government: Multiparty republic
Per capita GNP: U.S. $670

▶ The bright lights of Jakarta surround the Independence Monument on the densely populated island of Java. Jakarta, the capital of Indonesia, is the center of its industry, government, and business.

ENDANGERED WORLD
Orang utans are endangered because people are destroying the forests where they live.

◀ Workers bundle dried stems of rice into sheaves during harvest. Rice is the main food crop in Indonesia. The high levels of production have made it one of the world's leading rice producers.

511

INDONESIA *People and History*

The first people to live here probably came from mainland Malaysia. From about A.D. 700, the islands' wealth of spices and their position on important trade routes drew seafarers from many other nations. Indian merchants brought the Hindu religion, and Arab traders brought Islam.

During the 1500s and 1600s, the Portuguese and British struggled to control the islands, but it was the Dutch who succeeded in 1798. Under Dutch rule the islands developed a sense of unity. They fought for independence and declared Indonesia a republic in 1949. Since independence, the army has been a powerful political force. It squashed a communist rebellion in 1965 and occupied East Timor during a rebellion in 1975. Two leaders have dominated recent history. The independent nation's first president was Achmed Sukarno, who gave Indonesians a real feeling of national identity. A military coup led to a takeover by General Suharto, who has encouraged greater political and religious tolerance.

▲ *Schoolchildren play outside their classroom in Bali. Many learn English and Bahasa Indonesia, the national language, at school. Children usually speak their island's regional dialect at home.*

A fast-growing population means that poverty is a problem on the islands, even though the government has increased food production, industry, and health care. Most Indonesians are farmers and some practice "slash and burn" agriculture—cutting down the forest and moving on once the soil is exhausted. Indonesian life is filled with ancient traditions drawn from Buddhist, Hindu, and folk sources, even though most people are Muslims. Each island follows its own customs.

◀ *This ruined Buddhist temple, on the island of Java, has 72 bell-shaped structures that contain stone sculptures of Buddha. Buddhism was once an important religion on the islands, but few Indonesians follow it today.*